Triumph Spitfire and GT6

Triumph Spitfire and GT6

A collector's guide
by Graham Robson

MOTOR RACING PUBLICATIONS LTD
Unit 6, The Pilton Estate, 46 Pitlake, Croydon CR0 3RA, England

First published 1991

British Library Cataloguing in Publication Data

Robson, Graham
  Triumph Spitfire & GT6.
  I. Title
  629.2222

ISBN 0-947981-60-8

Typeset by Ryburn Typesetting Ltd; origination by
Ryburn Reprographics, Halifax, West Yorkshire

Printed in Great Britain by
The Amadeus Press Limited, Huddersfield, West Yorkshire

Contents

Like the front cover illustration, this picture of an immaculate GT6 and a painstakingly restored Spitfire was taken by Peter Williams, General Secretary of The Triumph Sports Six Club.

Introduction

The Triumph Spitfire was a car of which Standard-Triumph could be proud. It was developed on a tiny budget, it came from engineers who had no previous experience of producing small sports cars, and it was a great and lasting success, which sold well for 18 years. That's why I am so pleased to have written this *Collector's Guide*, 30 years after serious development work began.

According to tradition, the Spitfire should never have been as good as it was, and here's why. Some companies take ages to build a reputation; very few leap straight into the limelight. Until 1953, Standard-Triumph wasn't even in the sports car business, yet within 10 years Triumph had become a famous name, a head-to-head competitor against the long-established MG company, particularly in the USA, where most sports cars were sold – and where the Spitfire had arrived.

Even if I had never had a direct connection with the development of the Triumph Spitfire and the GT6, I *know* I would always have been a great enthusiast for the range. In fact, when the car was being developed I was employed at Standard-Triumph, so when the opportunity arose in 1964, I was very happy to buy a Spitfire. In recent years I have never missed an opportunity to drive and ride in these pretty machines.

There was a time when I would have had to say that these were underrated cars, but now there is no need. Now that most classic car enthusiasts know that the Spitfire always outsold its deadly rival, the Sprite/Midget, and that the cars were more attractive, more spacious and easier to maintain than the cars from Abingdon, there is no need to shout too loudly. The curvaceous Triumphs are no longer underrated, for their classic values and the restoration expertise is developing all the time.

My publisher John Blunsden has been very generous with the space allowed in this *Collector's Guide*, so I hope I have been able to relate almost every detail, and every tiny nuance, of the life and times of these cars. When I was young, and working on prototypes and competition Spitfires, I was perennially fascinated by the cars. Today, 30 years later, I still am.

July 1991   Graham Robson

Acknowledgements

There have to be limits – I genuinely find it impossible to include the name of every Triumph personality, or expert, who has helped me increase my knowledge of these cars over the years because there have been so many. In the context of the Spitfire and this book, here are the most important personalities:

I couldn't have written it without Harry Webster's help. Not only is he the engineer who led the original design team, but he was also the man whose vision saw the cars race at Le Mans. When I ran Standard-Triumph motorsport during the 1960s, he indulged many of my whims – and, more important, he understood them. In later years he gave me a lot of background information, and is still genuinely proud of these cars.

John Lloyd was Harry's deputy and, for several years, my boss at Standard-Triumph. As far as I could see he was neither a sports car nor a sporting enthusiast, but he was the calmest and the kindest of managers.

Once again it was my American colleague Richard Langworth who helped me with information and encouragement from the United States. Without Richard, I would continue to think of the USA as a colony...

Anders Clausager, BMIHT's eminent archivist, provided yet more production data to add to that which I had collected over the years. When it comes to quoting numbers and dates, Anders and I are agreed that factories never keep enough of the right sort of information – and that no two sources agree. We also agree that the figures I quote in the following pages are the most accurate available today...

I reserve special thanks for the staff of the Triumph Sports Six Club at Lubenham, Market Harborough. John Griffiths, Peter Williams, Bill Sunderland, Trudi Squibbs and Bernard Robinson allowed me to disrupt their days, and all helped a lot.

Graham Robson

CHAPTER 1

Ancestors and heritage

Standard Ten and Herald

I cannot think of a single mass-produced sports car which was designed without compromise. The Triumph Spitfire, like the MG Midget, the Austin-Healey 100, the Fiat X1/9 and the Alfa Romeo Spider, could never have been built without the existence of one or more successful family cars. The Spitfire, in fact, was closer to the Triumph Herald than the TR4 – and without the dumpy little Standard 10 it might never have happened.

To be economically viable, such cars had to be developed by plundering the corporate 'parts bin'. Publicists don't like to admit it, but glamorous sports cars never sell in numbers high enough to justify the development of special new running gear. Quite simply, most sports cars would never have been developed if they could not pick up engines, transmissions and suspension units from mundane (sometimes quite horrid) family machines.

Well before the Spitfire was even thought of, there was a lot of history behind this tradition. The original MG Midget of 1928 had been Morris Minor-based, and made money. The PA and PB Midgets were much more specialized and were loss-makers. By contrast, the TA which replaced it looted the Morris parts bin – and was profitable.

After World War Two, no design team ever forgot that. The Jaguar XK120 used running gear intended for the Mk VII saloon, the TR2 used a lot of Standard Vanguard hardware, the Austin-Healey Sprite relied heavily on the Austin A35, while the Chevrolet Corvette leaned heavily on the Bel Air for its inspiration.

So it was with the Spitfire. Although the Spitfire was launched in 1962, the story *really* began to unfold in 1950...

Triumph and Standard

Triumph, of course, had originally been founded in 1887 to make pedal cycles, had made its first motorcycles in 1902, and its first cars in Coventry in 1923. The company over-expanded in the 1930s, making several fine sports cars along the way, but collapsed financially in 1939, and the rights to its name (but little else) were bought up by the Standard Motor Company Ltd in 1944. Standard, also of Coventry, had been in the car business since 1903, and was one of the British motor industry's 'Big Six', with its major facility at Canley, on the western outskirts of Coventry.

Thereafter, cars with the Triumph badge were *really* Standard-Triumphs, for not a single prewar component survived to be used on postwar models. Although Standard's despotic managing director, Sir John Black, wanted to use the Triumph marque badge to make an assault on his business rival, William Lyons, at Jaguar, he made little progress at first.

Until the early-1950s, in fact, Standard's sporting marque had a rather uneasy existence. The first Standard-Triumphs were tubular-chassis machines using prewar Flying Standard running gear, while the second (the Mayflower) was an odd attempt to use so-called razor-edge styling on a stubby wheelbase, with a mixture of Standard Flying Ten and Standard Vanguard running gear. Purists still shudder at the thought, even today. The bulbous TRX Roadster of 1950 was later cancelled. For Triumph, things only began to look

The first sporting Triumph built by Standard was the 1800 Roadster, which had a tubular frame and Standard 14 running gear. It was large, heavy and slow – not at all like the Spitfire which was to come.

up in the mid-1950s, when the famous TR sports cars came on the scene.

'SC' – Standard's new small car

For the first three years after World War Two, Standard's only small car was the 1930s-style Standard Flying Eight model, which had a 28bhp 1-litre side-valve engine. Then, after a pause, the 38bhp 1.25-litre Triumph Mayflower took

over; it was too expensive, too ugly and too late.

In 1950, therefore, Sir John Black ordered technical director Ted Grinham (a man with no interest in the design and driving of sporting cars) to start a new small car project. With a stunning lack of invention, this became known as the 'SC' (Small Car) project.

Right from the start, Sir John made it clear that it was to be very low-priced, that it had to compete head-on with the

Morris Minor and the forthcoming Austin A30, and that there were to be no frills.

By the end of 1951 the layout of SC was settled. It was to be new from stem to stern, and although the price targets were tough, original thoughts of giving it a side-valve engine and a three-speed gearbox were abandoned. The three-speed 'box option was only finally killed nine months before production began.

Fisher & Ludlow (soon to be absorbed by the British Motor Corporation) got the contract to produce the unit-construction body monocoque at Tile Hill, in the outskirts of Coventry. The first type to go on sale was a simple little four-door saloon (it was only 11ft 10in long and had no exterior boot access), though estate car and van derivatives would soon follow.

The new car, titled Standard Eight, was launched in September 1953. The engine was a rugged little cast-iron four-cylinder unit of only 803cc. With a combined inlet and exhaust manifold casting and a 26mm Solex downdraught carburettor, peak power was only 26bhp (gross) at 4,500rpm,

The Standard Eight was launched in 1953 and was soon joined by the Standard Ten. These were the first cars to use the engines and gearboxes which were further developed for Spitfire use in the 1960s.

'Big Brother' – the famous Triumph TR3A – was built from 1957 to 1961 and confirmed Standard-Triumph's new reputation for building fast, value-for-money sports cars.

and maximum torque was 39lb/ft at 2,800rpm. That sounds terribly puny, but it was absolutely competitive with BMC's A-Series-engined A30s and Morris Minors. One feature of the engine which would be regretted in later years was that it had only two inlet ports – cylinders 1 & 2 and 3 & 4 each sharing a siamesed port.

The gearbox was also brand new, a compact little four-speed unit with wide ratios, no bottom-gear synchromesh and a long direct-acting central change-speed lever. At the rear was a new hypoid-bevel rear axle with a 4.875:1 final-drive ratio.

A few months later the Eight was joined by the Ten, this being the same basic car, but with a larger-bore 948cc engine, a better cylinder-head, 33bhp at 4,500rpm and 46lb/ft of torque at 2,500rpm, a 4.55:1 final-drive ratio, external access to the boot, and a more completely equipped interior.

With these two cars Standard-Triumph (under its new and still-young managing director Alick Dick) mightily expanded its sales, and continued to improve the specification and output of the engines and the cars they powered. Then, in the autumn of 1957, the company announced the Standard Pennant. At first sight this was no more than a facelifted Standard Ten, but a lot of detailed new engineering was hidden under the skin.

The bodyshell had been treated to new front and rear wings, with hooded headlamps and small rear fins, and there was a new facia. Mechanically, the 948cc. engine had been given a 28mm-choke carburettor, and now produced 39bhp at 5,000rpm, but the most important improvement was to give the gearbox a new remote-control linkage and a stubby gear-lever.

Standard's Eight, Ten and Pennant formed a trio of very saleable little cars – but by this time greater and more exciting things were on the way. Standard-Triumph was already developing a successor, which was due to take over in 1959.

Triumph Herald – a troubled beginning
Standard-Triumph had started thinking about a new

Stripping a Triumph Herald chassis for inspection after one of its early proving runs in Spain. This chassis was the ancestor of the one to be used in the Spitfires and GT6s.

'Turn left for Tangier.' The two trans-African Herald prototypes and the Pennant estate car which was their tender vehicle refuel in deepest Africa.

A 1959 Herald demonstrates the incredible turning circle of all cars in this family. The same feature was included in the Spitfire specification.

generation of small cars in March 1956 – coding them 'Zobo' – but before major decisions could be taken there were two important obstacles to be cleared away. One concerned the supply of body monocoques, the other was over styling.

Although the two were interlinked, the question of supply was paramount. In the 1950s, as in the 1940s, Standard-Triumph had no in-house body plant which could stamp out huge numbers of unit-construction shells. The Mulliners factory in Birmingham (which Standard-Triumph was to take over in 1958) was more suited to building tens of thousands of shells for the TR3, or for modifying SC underpans for vans and estates.

For the SC it had been happy to place its business with Fisher & Ludlow, but since then F & L had been absorbed by one of Standard-Triumph's rivals, BMC. When Alick Dick asked BMC's abrasive chairman Sir Leonard Lord if F & L would build the SC's successor, he was abruptly and rudely turned away. When he approached the only viable alternative – Pressed Steel of Cowley, near Oxford – he was politely told to join a lengthy queue!

Since there was no question of settling the style until the supply of shells could be assured, Alick Dick's team thought again. This was probably just as well, for the in-house stylists seemed to be incapable of coming up with an attractive shape.

There was another, relatively new, factor. More and more British cars were being assembled from kits in overseas factories in countries like India, South Africa and Australia. Any new car would have to take account of this.

In the end, the problem was solved in two ways, both with the same aim. One was for the engineers to take the *very* brave step of reverting to a separate chassis-frame; the other was to use it as a self-supporting jig to build up the shell from large sections.

It was a brilliant solution which always worked well as long as the cars were carefully and correctly assembled. The separate chassis-frames doubled perfectly as jigs, and made overseas assembly much more simple than before. The ability to build the body from sections meant that each section could be ordered from a smaller body-maker, and one of Alick

Dick's immediate objectives was to tie-up such firms – or even take them over – as rapidly as possible.

There was another advantage. By using what we might now call a modular type of construction, Standard-Triumph could build a greater variety of styles without investing too much capital. As well as saloons, estate cars and vans, why not consider making coupes, pick-ups and – who knows? – sports cars...

So far, so good. Next, to settle the on-going styling problem, Standard-Triumph contracted the brilliant young Italian Giovanni Michelotti to look after its future programme. After retouching the Standard Vanguard, he then turned his attention to 'Zobo'. Having been given a free hand to shape cars around a new 91.5in wheelbase chassis, Michelotti produced a startling series of sketches, which were instantly approved.

By the end of the 1950s the driving forces behind all new projects were Alick Dick, general manager Martin Tustin and technical chief Harry Webster. As early as August 1957 the minutes of a board meeting contained an analysis of the

This was the engine bay of an early-specification Triumph Herald, showing that the general layout of the Spitfire's front end was already established.

timing of the 'Zobo' project, projected the price of the family car versions and deferred detail consideration of 'a sports version' until a later date. What eventually became the Spitfire, therefore, was already being mentioned, even though no work had yet been done.

As every Triumph enthusiast knows, the Herald design was based on a rather flexible separate chassis, which had independent front *and* rear suspension and rack-and-pinion steering. The wishbone front suspension offered an incredibly tight steering lock, but rear suspension was by high-pivot swing-axles, which were apt to promote snap oversteer when pressed to the limit.

The first cars used developed versions of the Standard Ten/Pennant engine and gearbox, with a new chassis-mounted final-drive unit. The first Heralds used 35bhp or 45bhp 948cc engines, 4.875:1 or 4.55:1 axle ratios, and were built in two-door saloon or coupe form. At that time all of them had drum brakes, and there was no overdrive option,

The first open-air car in the Herald range was the convertible of 1960. It was bigger, more squarely styled and a lot heavier than the Spitfire would be. The fold-back soft-top, however, was a lot more luxuriously detailed than that of the future Spitfire.

This specially prepared exhibit showed the general proportions of the 948cc Triumph Herald twin-carb engine. With only minor development changes (and enlargement to 1,147cc) it proved to be suitable for the Spitfire which followed.

15

Worm's-eye view of the characteristic Herald/Spitfire/GT6 front suspension. This picture is of a Herald 1200 underside, and is printed to show how all the cars in this family used the same basic layout.

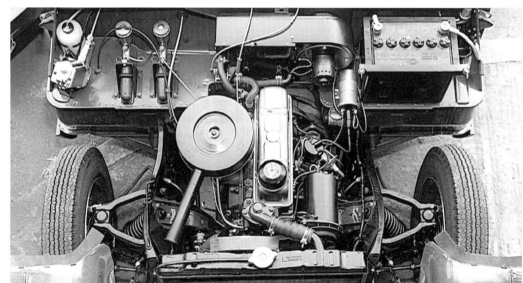

The Herald 1200's engine bay had metal splash-guards along its sides, and the engine only a single carburettor. Many features of this layout were adopted in modified form for the new Spitfire.

Close study of this shot proves that it was a twin-carb 948cc Triumph Herald engine, but the future links with the original 1,147cc Spitfire Mk 1 are obvious.

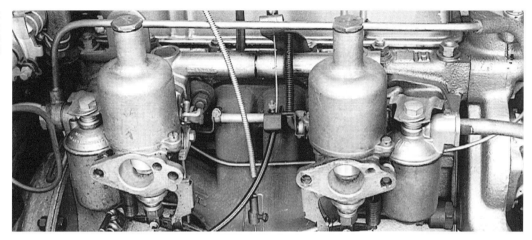

Two of the men who inspired the birth of the Spitfire – George Turnbull, at the wheel, with Harry Webster alongside him – pose in Spitfire prototype X692 in 1962.

even though this had latterly been available on the Eights, Tens and Pennants.

Critics soon made it clear that while they liked the design, they didn't like the build quality, and at a time when Standard-Triumph needed to sell every car it could make, demand began to drop away, such that bankruptcy soon appeared possible, and Alick Dick had to find a saviour. The result, announced at the end of 1960, was that Leyland Motors made a takeover bid, which was duly formalized in the spring of 1961.

For the Herald there was another problem, namely that the cars were rather heavier than originally hoped, and soon dealers and potential customers were begging for more performance. Harry Webster's engineers therefore managed to enlarge the willing little SC engine still further, producing a 39bhp (single-carburettor) and, later, a 51bhp (single-carburettor) 1,147cc unit, which was ready for launch in 1961.

The Herald 1200 range – saloon, coupe, estate car, convertible and van – was Triumph's definitive small car

When Leyland took over Standard-Triumph in 1961, it installed Stanley Markland to make sense of the financially ailing business. Markland is behind the wheel of this Vitesse, with Triumph's technical chief Harry Webster talking to him.

In my opinion this was the best-handling Herald of all time – I drove it often. In fact it was a short-wheelbase car of Spitfire length – note the use of shortened doors – built to speed-up Spitfire development.

The Herald coupe, seen here in sectioned show guise, was a true forerunner of the Spitfire. This particular shot shows the packaging of the chassis, transmission and floorpan, which would be used in modified form for the Spitfire. Those rear seats were perfectly usable as long as one was not too tall.

This was the first type of six-cylinder engine to be installed in the Herald type chassis – the 1.6-litre version which powered the Vitesse. For use in the GT6 a 2-litre version of exactly the same bulk would be used.

This is the Vitesse 1600 engine ready to be installed in the chassis. Obviously it is longer, though no wider or higher than the four-cylinder Herald unit.

statement for the 1960s. It was faster, more flexible and above all better built than the original Herald, and it underpinned Standard-Triumph's fortunes for the next few years. Without the Herald, of course, there could have been no Spitfire.

'Atom' – six into four will go...

Every Triumph enthusiast knows that the Spitfire evolved from the Herald, just as they know that the GT6 evolved from the Vitesse. Once the engineers had discovered that it was *just* possible to shoehorn a Vanguard Six-type engine into the engine bay of a Herald, the 'Atom' project took shape, and that car was launched in 1962 as the Vitesse.

By the summer of 1962, therefore, Standard-Triumph had a much more modern range to sell, it was emerging from its financial traumas, the Heralds, Vitesses and TR4s were selling in ever-increasing numbers, and even the hard-headed businessmen from Leyland Motors had started to smile.

Now it was time for the next new model – the Spitfire.

CHAPTER 2

Spitfire 1, 2 and 3

Michelotti's masterpiece

Although Standard-Triumph's directors started talking about a new small sports car in 1957, it took more than five years to bring the attractive Spitfire to the market.

Why did it take so long? Two words sum up the delay – priorities, and money. Even though there were plenty of enthusiasts in Coventry who were keen to see the birth of a 'baby sister' for the successful TR, they had to get into a long queue behind other models.

When you consider Standard-Triumph's see-sawing finances in the 1958–1962 period, the flow of new products was amazing. Between the first mention of a 'Zobo sports car' in August 1957 and the launch of the Spitfire in October 1962, the following new models were introduced:

Standard Pennant
Standard Ensign
Triumph TR3A
Standard Atlas van
Triumph Herald
New 'Sabrina' 20X Le Mans racing engine
Standard Atlas Major
New six-cylinder engine
Standard Vanguard Six
Triumph Herald 1200
Triumph TR3B
Triumph TR4
Standard Ensign De Luxe
Triumph Vitesse 1600

In addition, the 'Zebu' large saloon and 'Zero' tractor projects were both designed, but later cancelled. It was no wonder that the Spitfire had to wait so long.

This is also the time to kill another legend – that the Spitfire was only produced as an answer to BMC's new Austin-Healey Sprite. The Sprite was launched in mid-1958, a year after the *original* 'Zobo sports car' had been discussed.

Although Standard-Triumph and BMC had been direct rivals for some time (Triumph TR versus Austin-Healey 100 was a perfect example), the Spitfire was not a knee-jerk reaction to the Sprite.

The appearance of the Sprite, however, was a great spur to Harry Webster's ambitions. Before the arrival of the Sprite, he thought his team could do a better job; *after* the launch, he was convinced of this!

Even so, it was not until the spring of 1960 that Alick Dick, Webster, Martin Tustin and George Turnbull, at that time production manager, were able to turn their attention to the new small sports car. Having coded it 'Bomb', they decided to lay down the bare bones of the design, and challenge Michelotti to produce an attractive style.

By this time Michelotti's work was renowned throughout the European motor industry, but this was the little Italian's first chance to shape a small sports car. In 1960, 'Bomb' would have to face up to the cheeky little Sprite (I haven't called it ugly, though others have), to the smart but somehow anonymous Fiat 1200 Cabriolet (by Pininfarina) and (in a higher price bracket) to the neat little Alfa Romeo Giulietta Spider (also by Pininfarina).

'Bomb', or X659, the very first Spitfire prototype as built by Michelotti, was delivered to Coventry in the autumn of 1960, then spent the first nine months of its life under a dust sheet before Leyland authorized development to begin.

This show-prepared chassis is actually of a Mk 2, in 1965, and demonstrates the neat backbone chassis-frame, which, allied to strong bodyshell sills, gave the Spitfire most of its strength.

This is only an installation check for the first Spitfire chassis-frame, so please do not get confused by the Herald 1200 engine and front brakes in this shot. From this angle the solid layout of the Spitfire's frame is obvious.

Before packaging work began in Turin, Standard-Triumph decided that 'Bomb' would have a tuned version of the new 1,147cc engine, an 83in wheelbase, and would retain the same front and rear suspension, plus rack-and-pinion steering, of the Herald. The frame, however, was not to be merely a shortened version of the Herald chassis, but to be a new backbone design complete with sturdy box-section members at each side of the power train.

Because this wheelbase was only 8.5in shorter than that of the Herald, it meant that 'Bomb' could have a roomy and comfortable two-seater cockpit; this was one of the many advances Webster was determined to offer over the Sprite. Independent road tests later revealed that the Spitfire had 5in more length in the passenger footwells, 3.5in more width

across the shoulders, as well as a generous amount of stowage space behind the seats.

By 1960, Standard-Triumph had reacted to early criticism of the Herald's body structure, where complaints centred on its flexibility, allied to tendencies to leak, creak and rattle. Although 'Bomb' would retain the very practical feature of a large, lift-up, front-end assembly (bonnet, front wings and wheelarches) hinged at the front of the chassis, the main bodyshell would all be welded, rather than bolted together.

Because the chassis itself was to be a backbone layout, the bodyshell was also given very strong sills (which replaced the side-members of the Herald), while the bulkhead area behind the seats was beefed-up to allow the rear suspension radius-arms to be bolted to it.

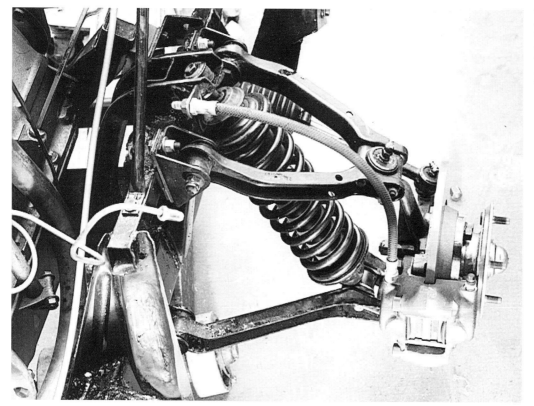

This is the well-known wishbone front suspension of the Herald/Vitesse/Spitfire/GT6 family showing the coil-over-damper installation, the wide-based bottom wishbone and the sturdy vertical link, which was used by several single-seater racing cars of the period.

Development deferred

At this time, Harry Webster was making regular weekend trips to and from Turin (usually driving the latest prototype which needed assessment), so he could closely monitor the progress of the new car. Michelotti submitted a range of styling suggestions and, once the preferred shape was chosen, began building a wooden buck on the basis of a chopped-down Herald chassis. It took time for Webster's needs to be satisfied, for he, the great enthusiast, wanted door sills to be cut down far enough for him to dangle his arms over the side and to touch the ground with his fingers.

Standard-Triumph supplied Michelotti with a 948cc-engined Herald coupe as a donor car, and the first 'Bomb' took shape in the summer and autumn of 1960. Although it lacked the smart facia and instrument panel of production cars, and the winding windows in the doors, the style would be little altered between then and the start-up of production in the autumn of 1962.

In the meantime, and to get some handling work done in advance, a suitably shortened-wheelbase Herald convertible (Commission No X661) was built in Coventry. Painted battleship grey, and with the most skimpy and disreputable of soft-top hoods, it was an enjoyable car to drive, but was never meant as a possible production car.

Like the original Heralds and Vitesses, the first Spitfires used simple high-pivot swing-axle rear suspension with a transverse leaf spring, which was bolted to the top of the rear axle casing.

Because Standard-Triumph was determined to produce a car with better equipment than the Sprite, 'Bomb' was given front disc brakes, wind-up windows and a separate lockable boot compartment; the original Sprite had none of these features, and it was not until October 1962 (the very month that Triumph's new car was launched) that disc brakes became available.

In the meantime, Standard-Triumph's finances were going from bad to worse, with money beginning to pour out of the business. Too much effort had gone into expansion, yet the Herald was not selling as fast as hoped, the Standard Vanguard and the Triumph TR3A were both dying rapidly, and the company's borrowings were reaching astronomical levels.

The result was that when the first 'Bomb' prototype (Commission No X659) was delivered to Coventry in October 1960, it was almost immediately covered in a dust sheet and put into storage. To save money on capital expenditure there was a freeze on new model tooling work, and at that time there seemed to be no chance of 'Bomb' ever

going into production.

Then came the rescue. Leyland Motors made a takeover bid for Standard-Triumph in December 1960, and took control early in 1961, but for several agonizing months the prototype sat in a corner of the experimental department, under its dust sheet, with no funds available for its development.

In the meantime, Leyland had seconded Stanley Markland (who was already works director of Leyland and managing director of Albion Motors) to work at Coventry. In all but name he was already running the Standard-Triumph business. It was on one of his periodic guided tours – a quick 'walk-through' of the experimental department – that he saw an intriguing shape under a dust sheet. In Harry Webster's own words:

"'What's that?', Stanley wanted to know, and when I whipped off the sheet to show him the 'Bomb' he instantly said, 'That's nice, what's it all about, and how far has it got?'.

"I told him that this was the single running prototype, that it was really more of a quick lash-up than the final design, but that it had been shelved for lack of funds.

"I shall never forget what happened next. He looked at it, he sat in it, he walked round it, then he turned to me and said, 'That's good. We'll make that'. He never even referred back to Sir Henry Spurrier or to Donald Stokes – he approved it personally, there and then."

'Bomb' into Spitfire – the first few years

Once Markland had made his decision, work on 'Bomb' went ahead rapidly. Board approval for production tooling came in July 1961, with Forward Radiator of Birmingham (a subsidiary of Mulliners Ltd) getting the contract to build bodyshells) and Sankeys being chosen to produce backbone chassis-frames.

Markland wanted to see the new car launched at the London motor show in October 1962, which meant that time was very short. The first true prototypes (X691 and X692, later registered 4305 VC and 412 VC, respectively) were not completed until spring 1962, and pavé and endurance testing was not complete until mid-summer.

No-one now remembers how 'Bomb' came to be named Spitfire, and although there was no intended connection with the famous World War Two fighter plane, this still gave invaluable photo opportunities in the months which followed.

The new car was introduced on October 17, 1962, going on sale at £730 with a 63bhp/1,147cc engine. Almost immediately there was a British purchase tax reduction, which saw the Spitfire priced at £641 at a time when Sprite/Midget specs and prices started at 55bhp, 1.1 litres and £587. Standard-Triumph thought it could easily live with such a price differential as it was offering a faster car with better equipment.

Only four cars were built in August and September 1962, but 139 followed in October, 421 in November and 725 in December. Monthly production passed the 1,250 mark in January 1963 and the Spitfire saga was well under way.

Although the original car was well-equipped for the period, it still featured a 'build-it-yourself' soft-top, there were rubber mats on the floor, the wheels only had 3.5in rims, and

The Spitfire Mk 1 made its public debut at the London motor show in October 1962. There were two cars on the Triumph stand, one of them on a turntable, with a Vitesse 1600 close behind.

Show exhibits of Spitfire rolling chassis made the Spitfire's Herald heritage very clear, for the whole of the front end was recognizably developed from this family car.

In side view the Spitfire had pleasant, flowing lines. The windscreen was shared with the TR4 model, and there was much more cockpit space than in most rival sports cars.

the heater was still a £13 extra.

Even though there were a number of desirable features which had not been built into the new car – the Vitesse close-ratio gears would have suited the car's character better, there was no wire wheel option at first, and no overdrive – *Motor* magazine still described the Spitfire as 'An outstanding new small sports car'. In other words, Standard-Triumph's pretty little sports car had got off to a good start.

For the next few years Standard-Triumph's problem was not to sell the cars it could build, but to build the cars its dealers had already sold. The Spitfire sold well in the USA

right from the start – 6,224 cars in 1963, 8,761 in 1964 and 9,097 cars in 1965. Dealers were delighted to have two very different models – Spitfire and TR4 – to sell, and in a few years, after the GT6 had arrived, the range was even better-balanced.

Because every subsequent Spitfire model was developed logically and directly from the original, I should now record the major base-line features of the 1963 model:

The 1,147cc engine had twin 1.25in-choke SU carburettors, a cast-iron exhaust manifold and a 9:1 compression ratio; it produced 63bhp and was a direct

Details for restorers. All the electrical fittings were standard, off-the-shelf, Joseph Lucas items, the grille mesh was used on other Triumph saloons of the day, while the T R I U M P H letters were all separately fixed to the bonnet pressing.

descendant of the twin-carb engine fitted to 948cc Heralds.

The four-speed gearbox had no synchromesh on first gear, was the same as that used in Herald 1200s, and was visually the same as that used in 948cc Heralds.

The final-drive was the same as that used in the Herald 1200, having the same 4.11:1 ratio.

Front and rear suspensions (coil-spring/wishbone, and transverse-leaf/swing-axles, respectively) were visually the same as used in Herald 1200s, but different spring and damper rates were used. To tune the handling as far as possible, Standard-Triumph recommended 18psi front and 24psi rear tyre pressures.

The rack-and-pinion steering and the 16in steering wheel were the same as used in the Herald 1200, with the too-low gearing of 3.8 turns lock to lock. Steering effort was low and the turning circle was a miraculous 24ft 2in between kerbs and 26ft 0in between walls, to quote *Autocar*'s road test, published on November 16, 1962.

For £641 in 1963 one got a car with a 92mph top speed, 0–60mph in about 17 seconds, and fuel economy in the 30–36mpg range. By comparison with today's Fiestas and Metros that doesn't sound exciting, but in 1962 it definitely made BMC sit up and take notice. *Autocar* testers thought that it was: 'a refined car with a number of advanced features...appropriately good performance and fuel economy.'

But what about the handling, which later became such an issue with pundits? There was criticism, albeit veiled, right from the start. *Autocar* testers thought the ride was too hard, tending to set up rattles and vibration, and 'The driver can detect...mild understeer changing to oversteer as the weight transfer affects the rear suspension. The car remains easy to control and has a wide safety margin for the over-enthusiastic. On wet roads adhesion is not good, and the back of the car is quick to slide...'

Motor, which sampled a different car, went further. 'Handling is safe and enjoyable. There is appreciable

The Spitfire Mk 1's cockpit was quite sparsely equipped, for there was moulded rubber carpet on the floor, the seats had no adjustment for rake, while the handbrake and steering wheel/column came directly from the existing Herald model.

The Spitfire Mk 1's facia/instrument panel was well-equipped, but a lot of painted metal was still on show. The two stowage trays were very useful, and there was provision for a radio to be fitted. The author fitted his own radio in less than a morning.

The original Spitfire had no splash-guards in the engine bay, but as a result access for all repairs and maintenance was unrivalled. The radiator header tank is above and inboard of the twin SU carburettors.

The Spitfire's boot was a very sensible size, but it was not very luggage-friendly. There were many exposed panel joints, trim was very bare, and the jack had to be stowed in the nearside wheelarch.

understeer giving stability in straight line running and during mild cornering, which changes gradually to a slight, controllable oversteer as the speed builds up. The transition takes place gently as the swing-axle i.r.s. changes to a positive camber. The result is that as the cornering limit is approached, the tail "hangs out" and a little steering has to be paid off, after which the chosen line will be followed closely. Long fast curves have to be approached with some caution until this changeover has been effected...'

For the moment, though, the car got a good reception, and the factory got on with the improvement process. From the autumn of 1963 three major new options arrived – a detachable steel hardtop, centre-lock wire wheels with 4.5in rims, and Laycock overdrive which operated on top and third gears. Only simple modifications were needed to make overdrive work on second and first gears as well, but the

From the autumn of 1963 it was possible to order a Spitfire with this neat rounded hardtop as an optional extra. Because the doors had wind-up windows this turned the little car into a snug two-seater coupe.

factory frowned on this.

In the meantime, and related to the Spitfire motorsport programme, three engine tune-up kits had rather reluctantly been put on sale, though one of them – Stage 1 – seems to have been unavailable! More to satisfy the homologation regulations than to establish a new market, these were as follows:

Interim included a high-compression (9.75:1) head, a downdraught Solex 32PAIA carburettor, a tubular exhaust manifold, and 70bhp. The cost was £47 16s 1d.

Stage I included an eight-port cylinder-head and a 10.5:1 compression ratio, different manifolds and camshaft timing, and 80bhp. Although the price was quoted at £92 5s 0d, the carburettor to be used was not specified, and I suspect none were ever sold!

Stage II was a serious replica of that used on the works cars, but still not as powerful. There was a 10.5:1-compression eight-port head (*not* the same casting as that used by the team cars, rather a developed version of that intended for use in the 1300 saloon of 1965), new inlet and exhaust manifolds, two twin-choke Weber Type 40DCOE carburettors and a different camshaft profile; 90bhp at 6,500rpm was claimed for this kit, which was priced at £179. Top speed was claimed to be 107mph, with 0–60mph in 10.6sec.

However, customers were also recommended to buy stronger pistons, connecting-rods, crankshaft, clutch *and* the Vitesse close-ratio gears! Few did, but it was easy to notch up the price of a complete Stage II Spitfire to £1,000 and beyond.

Who knows how many of each kit were sold (through SAH Accessories)? The factory never made any claims, though 100 Stage IIs were supposed to be built to meet homologation claims. I doubt if more than a handful survive to this day.

Spitfire Mk 2 and Mk 3
BMC introduced an improved Sprite/Midget model in 1964 (for the first time this car had wind-up windows), but Standard-Triumph was ready to respond with the Spitfire Mk 2 in March 1965.

The only way to pick a Mk 2 (this car) from a Mk 1 was by the different type of grille mesh, and the badging on the bootlid. On this particular car the optional extra wire-spoke wheels are a feature, while the owner has fitted a pair of wing mirrors.

Compared with the original, it had a slightly more powerful engine – 67bhp instead of 63bhp – this being achieved by using different manifolds and revised valve gear, and there was a diaphragm-spring clutch. In the cabin there were carpets on the floor, and most of the original exposed paintwork had been covered over by trim panels.

The price crept up a little – if a customer ordered a heater, a hardtop, overdrive and wire wheels (as many did), the total price was more than £820 – but it was still a very desirable specification, which sold very well indeed.

Only two years later it was time for another change, this time with more substantial improvements. Compared with the Mk 2, the Spitfire Mk 3 had styling improvements, a larger engine and higher performance. It was exactly what Standard-Triumph needed to counter the latest competition from BMC, where the Spridget models had been given a 1.3-litre engine from the autumn of 1966.

The Spitfire Mk 3 went into production early in 1967, but to give the shipping 'pipeline' to the USA time to fill up, it was not launched until March. The most obvious change was that a new front bumper had been fitted, higher than before, so that it spanned the front grille opening; the most *important*, on the other hand, was that the engine had been enlarged to 1.3 litres.

The new engine capacity, in fact, was 1,296cc (the increase was achieved by providing a 73.7mm instead of

Mk 3 Spitfires (1967 to 1970) had a new type of bumper blade, which was several inches higher off the ground than before. Although it partly obscured the radiator entry ducts, there never seemed to be any cooling problems.

69.3mm cylinder bore), the cylinder-head was a mass-production version of the eight-port design first seen on the racing Spitfires in 1964 (but the two castings were completely different), and peak power was quoted at 75bhp at 6,000rpm. SU carburettors with 1.25in chokes had been retained, but there were new cast inlet and exhaust manifolds; the tubular manifold used on Mk 2 models had been abandoned because it was too expensive to produce.

Except that larger front brake calipers were specified, and that the electrical system was henceforth to be negative-earth, the only other noticeable change was that the TR4's 15in sprung-spoke steering wheel was now fitted. The raised front bumper had been fitted to allow the car to meet new USA safety legislation.

This was the first Spitfire to have a permanently fitted soft-top, where the folding frame and the soft-top itself could be folded back into the tail and hidden under a pouch without the lines being destroyed. Apart from this, the cockpit was virtually unchanged, though the instrument panel itself was given a wooden veneer finish.

Although British-market road test cars could not reach 100mph, *Road & Track* recorded 100mph for a US-specification model, where the Spitfire Mk 3 comfortably outpaced the 1967-model MG Midget with which it was being compared. In that year, as in 1968 and 1970, the Spitfire comfortably outsold the combined might of Sprite and Midget models.

By this time, though, the motoring press was definitely divided in its opinion of the Spitfire's rear suspension. *Autocar* wrote in 1969 '...we make no apology for referring to its handling limitations. Its stablemates, the GT6 and Vitesse, now have a completely redesigned rear suspension system. What a pity the Spitfire has not been included...'

In 1967 *Motor* had recorded: '...when trying *really* hard, as on a deserted roundabout into which the car is thrown with exuberance, or a favourite bend for which the car is set up beforehand, the initial understeer changes rapidly and sharply to strong oversteer as the jacking effect of the swing-axle rear suspension sets the wheels at undesirable camber angles...'

Before Standard-Triumph could respond to these sort of comments, its corporate world had changed. Owned by Leyland Motors since 1961, it had already seen that company buy up Rover (who already owned Alvis) in 1966/1967, but in January 1968 came the biggest merger of all – Leyland effectively took over British Motor Holdings, which not only included Jaguar-Daimler but the whole of the BMC complex.

This was the occasion of the foundation of British Leyland, a corporation launched amid many fine words at the time, but one which struck storm after financial storm in the years which followed. At a stroke, too, Standard-Triumph found itself owned by the same company which owned Austin-Healey and MG. Would the rivalry have to stop? Which marques would benefit in the future?

One result of the massive merger was a shake-up of personnel. Technical chief Harry Webster was drafted to Longbridge to knock some sense into Austin-Morris' engineering department, and his place at Coventry was taken by Rover's engineering genius Spen King.

The Mk 3 ran from 1967 to the autumn of 1970, but there

LON 897F was a famous British concours Spitfire Mk 3 in the 1970s and 1980s and was owned by Roger Rowley and his wife Anne.

This March 1967 publicity shot from Standard-Triumph shows the Mk3 complete with its raised bumper blade, which was ahead of the radiator grille mesh. Apart from this, the only other external visual change was to the tail, where new badges were fitted. The inside of the car was better and more tastefully equipped than before.

were two important development changes along the way. One came at the end of 1968, when, for the North American market only, the cars were given an entirely new instrument panel layout (we shall learn more about this in Chapter 3). The other came at the end of 1969, when all cars were given a mid-life 'freshen-up' pack which included the fitment of 4.5in disc wheels (to match the 4.5in rim wire-wheel options), a more sporty style of steering wheel, extra cockpit padding, a matt black windscreen surround, and a detachable rear window panel from the soft-top assembly.

The Mk 3 finally dropped out of production at the end of 1970, by which time its UK retail price had risen to £876, or £912 if the hardtop was specified. If a heater, overdrive and wire wheels were also specified, the price broke through the psychological £1,000 barrier.

Now it was time for a complete rethink.

Spitfire – versus – Spridget

Once the Spitfire was on sale there was no doubt that it only had one direct rival – the BMC Sprite/Midget model, which was being built at Abingdon, near Oxford. From 1962 to 1979 the cars fought head-to-head, and it is interesting to plot the way that the innovations swung one way, then another:

Year	Triumph	BMC
1956		Sprite conceived
1957	'Zobo sports' conceived	
1958		Sprite announced
1961		Sprite II/MG Midget announced
1962	Spitfire announced	Sprite/Midget 1100 launched
1964		Sprite III/Midget II announced
1965	Spitfire 2 announced	
1966		Sprite IV/Midget III announced
1967	Spitfire 3 announced	
1970	Spitfire IV announced	
1971		Sprite dropped
1974	Spitfire 1500 announced	Midget 1500 announced
1979	Midget 1500 dropped	
1980	Spitfire 1500 dropped	

This is the moment, too, to emphasize that from 1963 to 1979 the Spitfire outsold the Sprite/Midget models in every year except 1969, when Spitfire assembly was affected by a strike.

CHAPTER 3

Spitfire IV and 1500

Better handling, smoother style

Although the Spitfire Mk IV was eventually introduced in October 1970, work had been ticking over on the project since 1967. As in the early-1960s, when 'Bomb' became Spitfire, other priorities and influences had to be respected along the way.

First there was the enormous upheaval which followed the formation of British Leyland in 1968. Months of discussion, lobbying, rumours and special pleading surrounded a future product plan. Would Triumph or MG sports cars take precedence in the future? Would future designs carry more than one badge? Would the cars be built at Canley, Abingdon, or somewhere else?

As far as the Spitfire was concerned, by the late-1960s the original body press tooling was rapidly wearing out. As ever, new tools *could* encourage the design of reshaped panels, but should they? Was it time for a completely new shape, or merely for a facelift? Was it all financially justified? What was the likely effect of proposed North American legislation?

What was to be done about the Spitfire's engine? Future USA exhaust emission regulations were likely to hit hard at power and torque outputs – how could Triumph fight that? Could the ageing SC engine be further improved? Would the brand new Triumph slant-4 'Saab' overhead-cam engine fit, and if so was it viable?

What was to be done about the Spitfire's rear suspension to cure the wheel-jacking problem and the snap oversteer? Should the complex GT6 Mk 2 lower-wishbone system be adopted, or was there a simpler way?

Spen King, who took over from Harry Webster as technical director in the spring of 1968, took time to decide on the Spitfire's future. At the time his priorities were to get the TR6 into production, to finish development work on the new overhead-camshaft engines (slant-4 and V8 types), to finalize the restyled Mk 2 version of the Triumph 2000, and to sort out the complex new small car range of Toledo, 1500 and Dolomite 1850.

Shaping the Mk IV

In the meantime, Michelotti and Triumph's styling department were told that they could get together to consider a major facelift to the Spitfire's body, although they were told that the existing centre-section had to be retained. This, effectively, was the genesis of the Mk IV Spitfire and GT6 Mk 3.

In 1968, therefore, a new-style Spitfire took shape in the studios, one in which there was a smoother rear-end with the cut-off type of tail which was soon to be seen on the TR6, the 2.5 Mk 2 and the Stag, and in which a smoother nose included a droop-snoot bonnet with flip-up headlamps (Lotus Elan-style) mounted inboard of new wing/bonnet crown lines, and a wide and nicely detailed front grille. The screen was enlarged and the wiper pivots repositioned to suit.

Photographs of the flip-up headlamp style have survived, this being the car which was shown to the directors in December 1968, but no such car was ever put into production. Why? The answer, in a phrase, was USA legislation. By that time *proposed* laws seemed likely to outlaw flip-up headlamps in the 1970s. Because of the time-lag

This picture is dated September 1965 and shows how Standard-Triumph designers would have liked to restyle the nose of the Spitfire, using a flip-up headlamp design. Only one such mock-up car was ever produced, which was a pity.

involved between approving a scheme, getting it into production, and then the possibility of having to change back to a fixed-headlamp scheme (which might have looked as awful as the original 'frog-eye' Sprite) it was turned down.

As we now know, such laws were never enacted, though the threat was also enough to frighten other manufacturers, notably Ferrari, which produced a different version of the shark-nose Daytona for sale in the USA. For the Spitfire, Michelotti and the stylists were told that the rear-end restyle was fine (there was much more boot capacity than before), but that they should try again at the front.

The tragedy of all this was that the new shape was smooth,

attractive, practical, well-liked and could have been tooled without much delay or undue expense. In its place, a new front-end was produced which was smoother in detail, in fact with all-new panelling, but which looked much the same as earlier types.

The new style, which would grace the Mk IV and the 1500 models, was almost a complete reskin, but was clearly an update of the original Spitfire, and it got rid of the turned-out panel joints which had distinguished the original car. Even the door skins were different, and incorporated recessed door handles. For the first time there was to be a complete rear bumper (instead of two quarter-bumpers), and up front the bumper, bonnet and lower panel were more smoothly integrated than before, with the grille being under rather than behind the bumper.

This was also the opportunity to produce a new and more angular hardtop assembly, which featured a near-flat rear window and triangular-shaped quarter-windows behind the normal door glasses. The whole car, including its exposed-nut new-style road wheels, looked neat, businesslike and fresh enough to be sold for some years to come. At the time, however, no-one knew that this shape of Spitfire would be on sale for a full 10 years.

The introduction of the Mk IV was also the moment to specify the latest facia/instrument panel for all markets. Independent testers described this as a vast improvement –

for the first time on Spitfires the panel placed the speedometer and the rev-counter ahead of the driver's eyes, rather than in the centre of the car. The steering wheel had three polished alloy spokes, and was the same as that used in late-model Mk 3s.

Mk IV – revising the chassis
For the new Mk IV, the 1.3-litre engine was only lightly modified (in fact it seems to have been slightly *less* powerful than the Mk 3, but as the peak figures were quoted in 'DIN' rather than nett measure, we can only deduce this from road test results...), but this time it was backed by a new all-synchromesh gearbox.

This box, while developed from the old-style assembly and

The Spitfire Mk IV had a much smarter facia style than its predecessors, with the speedometer and rev-counter in front of the driver's eyes and with a wooden panel. This, in fact, was the 1973 'facelift' model, showing the alloy-spoked steering wheel which had been adopted by that time.

If you want proof that the swing-spring Spitfire Mk IV had been completely cured of rear wheel tuck-under tendencies, here is the proof...

The Spitfire Mk IV had a completely reskinned bodyshell, which not only featured an extended but cut-off tail and a near-flat bootlid, but bonnet seams moved down from the wing crown-line to the flanks (*and* turned in), as well as new door handles and locks. It was a very successful rework of what had always been a pretty design.

retaining many of the existing gears, bearings and synchromesh mechanisms, had a new and slightly longer casing and a different selector mechanism. The internal first-gear ratio was higher than before, as was the rear-axle ratio. Overdrive, which was still expected to be a popular option, was controlled by a sliding switch in the gear-lever knob. This box had also been developed for use in the new Toledo saloon, and in much-modified form would also soon find a home in the Morris Marina range.

The most important chassis improvement without question was to the rear suspension. Triumph had been tempted to adopt the very effective lower-wishbone system from the GT6 Mk 2, but instead chose a cheaper and simpler type of 'swing-spring' swing-axle layout.

This was ingeniously detailed, for when the car rolled on corners it allowed the centre of the transverse leaf spring to pivot on the top of the rear axle casing, a feature which kept the rear wheels nearly upright at all times and cancelled any tendency for them to jack-up and cause oversteer. To trim the balance of the suspension, a much stiffer front anti-roll bar was specified, and this was the first Spitfire to be sold with radial-ply tyres as standard.

Mk IV on sale – 1970 to 1974
It was typical of British Leyland's planning – eccentric, if not actually disorganized – that the launch of the Mk IV was

delayed until late October 1970, actually in the second week of the London motor show! More importantly, though, the Mk IV was meant as a 1971 model for the USA, where sales did not begin until the turn of the year.

As far as the British customer was concerned, the bad news was that the Mk IV cost more – £962, or £86 more than the last of the Mk 3s – but this had to be offset against the new style, the new gearbox and suspension, and the fact that the heater was now standard. The Spitfire was still more costly than the MG Midget, but the customers didn't seem to care, and in both the UK and the USA the Spitfire carried on winning the battle, by a comfortable margin.

Everyone agreed that it was a much nicer car. *Autocar*'s test ended with these words: 'Improvements on the Spitfire have made it a very much more civilised car, quieter and very pleasant to drive. The price, as tested, of £1,088.90, gives one a fast, good-handling sports car which now looks so much more refined than its predecessors.'

The same testers had enthused thus about the new car's handling: 'One of the most impressive things about the latest Spitfire is to be able to hurl it into a corner, lift off – and find the car still pointing where the driver aimed it. The initial understeer turns very gradually into virtually neutral handling, and only on the limit does a trace of oversteer make itself felt. It seems almost impossible now to get the back wheels to tuck under...'

Clearly, the reworking of the design, the restyle, and the investment in new tooling at Forward Radiator, had all been worthwhile, for the smooth new Mk IV remained in production at Canley for four years, during which more than 70,000 cars were built.

In those four years British customers were treated to very few changes or improvements, though there seemed to be a constant flow of modifications forced on to the cars sold in the USA. In 1972, radial-ply tyres (which had been a £10.45 option in 1971) became standard, but the most important improvements came early in 1973 when the Spitfire was given a 2in wider rear track (its entire swing-spring rear suspension being adopted at this time by the GT6 Mk 3), fire-retardant upholstery, reclining seats, a different steering

Later models of the Spitfire Mk IV, and all Spitfire 1500s, were fitted with an under-bumper chin spoiler.

wheel and instruments and a wooden-faced instrument panel.

Later in 1973 the centre-lock wire-wheel option was deleted; in August the original Laycock D-type overdrive was displaced by the new LH-type; before the end of the year an under-bumper front chin spoiler was standardized; and in 1974 the tonneau cover (which had cost £11.92 extra in 1971) was also standardized.

But this was the time when the whole world plunged towards a serious Energy Crisis, which may explain why UK sales slumped from 7,077 in 1972 to a mere 2,743 cars in 1974.

American-spec cars – throttled by legislation
American safety and exhaust emission regulations began to hit hard at the Spitfire from the end of the 1960s. The last of the USA-spec Mk 3s, the 1970 model, still produced 68bhp,

but needed a single Zenith-Stromberg carburettor to clean up its act.

That was bad enough, but with tighter regulations in 1971 the single-carb engine had to be detuned, to produce a mere 58bhp, and for 1972 that power sagged to a miserable 48bhp (nett); to maintain sports car performance, Triumph, in desperation, had to specify the old 4.11:1 rear axle instead of the 3.89:1 ratio.

For 1973 and 1974, with even tighter regulations in prospect, things looked so desperate that the factory had to ditch the old 1.3-litre engine and bring forward the first of the 1.5-litre engines in its place. These are described more fully later in the chapter   in this context, the single-carburettor engine restored peak power to 57bhp (nett), which allowed the 3.89:1 axle ratio to be re-adopted.

Fortunately for Triumph, every rival manufacturer was also

suffering badly, so a loss in performance by the Spitfire was matched by a similar loss from the Midget. In April 1973, a *Road & Track* Group Test in the USA showed that the Spitfire was still more powerful than the Midget, and that the performance of the two cars was almost identically matched.

Not only that, but at the end of the day, when assessing the cars' suitability for use in SCCA racing, the team summarized: 'For those who must win in Showroom Stock, the GT6 is most likely to do it. For fun, the Spitfire...the Midget won't win races because it doesn't go fast...'

Spitfire 1500 – the final modification

By the early-1970s the Triumph marque was submerged in British Leyland's corporate planning. From 1972 Triumph had been linked with Rover in design and business terms, and British Leyland bosses also wanted to avoid future conflict between Triumph and MG on the sports car front.

This meant that the Spitfire's future was no longer shaped at Canley, but in the ivory towers (some say in the cloud cuckoo land) of British Leyland management. If the money and the time had been available, Spen King's engineers would have liked to respond to the challenge of the mid-engined Fiat X1/9, but there were so many other projects to be tackled that this was never done.

At this time British Leyland saw only one way for its sports car businesses to stay viable; all new and existing models had

A study in noses. This group of Spitfires had been assembled for a Triumph Sports Six Club meeting. The car closest to the camera is a 1500, next is a Mk 3, and all are striving for concours awards.

The 1500 was in production from 1974 to 1980, selling very well indeed (and always outselling the MG Midget) until the end. The smooth lines of the tail and the large boot area are emphasized in this overhead shot.

to be optimized for sale in North America, and it could no longer consider making two distinctly different versions of the same car.

This meant that work to meet wave after wave of new legislation had to take precedence over more desirable developments, and all types had to be based on the same basic engine. It was going to be time-consuming and expensive, and it explains why neither the Spitfire nor the Midget were ever replaced. It also explains why no serious effort was ever made to re-engineer the car to accept the modern slant-4 overhead-cam engine, as already specified for the Saab 99, Dolomite and TR7 models.

Perhaps this explains why British Leyland seemed to snub the wishes and feelings of British and European enthusiasts in

the early-1970s, by having to keep the Spitfire, to make it heavier and somehow less sporty.

The new 'Bullet' (later TR7) project took up a lot of design time in the early-1970s, but to follow that British Leyland then decided to modernize the Spitfire and the Midget at the same time. With the USA market in mind, it was decided to have them share the same engine and gearbox from 1975 onwards!

But which engine and which gearbox? The important factor here was that the Midget's existing 1.3-litre A-Series was at the end of its development life, and its gearbox lacked synchromesh on first gear. Accordingly, Triumph came out on top of this competition, and in 1975 MG fanatics were enraged to see that their Midget was fitted with a Triumph

The Spitfire 1500's engine looked much like previous engines used in these cars, but there was a water-cooled inlet manifold, and the air cleaner pressing carries a plate with the 'British Leyland UK Ltd' insignia to emphasize who was now calling all the shots at Coventry.

Spitfire engine and a modified version of the Spitfire's transmission! In fact the Triumph-engined Midget was launched in October 1974, several weeks before the equivalent Spitfire was born.

Future USA exhaust emission regulations were going to squeeze engine outputs further, because sadly, to reduce exhaust emissions at this time, it was necessary to detune the engines. Even the UK-market engine's power had drooped from 63bhp to 61bhp in 1972. To restore the Spitfire's performance to a competitive level it would be necessary to enlarge or change the engine; fortunately for Triumph, the existing SC engine could still be stretched a little further.

When the original Herald 1200 engine had been developed, by a clever reshuffling of the cylinder bore centres, Triumph knew that some extra 'stretch' still remained, and when the 1.3-litre version was developed it had only been necessary to enlarge those bores. But this brought the bores to their largest practicable dimension, and the only way to make the 1.3-litre engine bigger was to lengthen the stroke.

Fortunately, the engineers had already done this on the closely related six-cylinder engine, so enlarging the four-cylinder SC engine was a straightforward process. When the 'six' was enlarged from 2 to 2.5 litres, for use in the TR5 sports car and 2.5PI saloon, the stroke had been increased from 76mm to 95mm. On the four-cylinder version, the stroke was increased from 76mm to 87.5mm, which meant that the capacity went up from 1,296cc to 1,493cc. This size of engine found its first home in South African-built Triumph saloons at the end of the 1960s, and it was then adopted for the front-wheel-drive Triumph 1500 saloon in 1970. A prototype 1.5-litre-engined Spitfire had been built and tested as early as 1966 – there is nothing like having future developments ready a few years in advance!

For 1975, therefore, the Spitfire Mk IV gave way to the Spitfire 1500; purists will point out that the 1973 and 1974 USA-market cars were really Spitfire 1500s, too, but Triumph never gave them that title.

For the 'Rest of the World' market (everywhere except North America) the Spitfire 1500 was to have a 1,493cc

A comparison of this Spitfire 1500 facia picture with that published on page 41 confirms that few major changes were made to Spitfire facias during the 1970s.

engine complete with twin SU carburettors, a cast exhaust manifold and a 9:1 compression ratio. In that form it was rated at 71bhp (DIN) and looked visually almost identical to the old 1.3-litre engine. Although the new engine was 15% larger than before, the peak power was 10bhp (or 16%) higher; this was quite enough to give the car a genuine top speed of 100mph.

Although the specification sheets confirmed that the gearbox ratios were the same as before, the 'box design itself was considerably different in detail. A new type of casing, allied to a different single-rail selector mechanism, had been developed for corporate use. This was already fitted to the Morris Marina, and was therefore adopted by the new Spitfire.

At the same time the back axle's final-drive ratio was raised to 3.63:1, this being the same as used in Morris Marina and Triumph Dolomite 1850 saloons.

Visually, the 1500 looked almost exactly like the Mk IV which it replaced, for the shape of the car was unchanged. To give the new customer something to boast about, though,

there were stylish new 'Spitfire 1500' decals on the bonnet and bootlid panels, along with a few other minor decoration changes.

By this time British Leyland was in such a state of paranoic chaos that the Spitfire received a muddled, not to say totally disorganized, introduction. The existing Mk IV model was exhibited at its 'native' show – Earls Court – in mid-October 1974, but three weeks later the Spitfire 1500 appeared, without fanfare, at the Turin motor show in Italy.

No press material was available at that time, and British Leyland publicists made no attempt to spell out what was going on. Perhaps this explains why *Motor*'s report missed it altogether, and why *Autocar* merely commented: 'This is a logical development, but British Leyland say that for the time being it is not for the home market.'

Charitably, I can only assume that spokesmen were stalling to allow the export pipeline to the USA to fill up (but since the 1975 USA-market model was virtually unchanged from 1974 I cannot see why...). Whatever, the official UK launch was delayed until early December.

The establishment press made much of the mechanical changes, though *Autocar* completely missed the arrival of the new gearbox. All correspondents seemed to find the new package even more attractive than before.

In the UK, the new car was priced at £1,509 (£1,553 if the hardtop was specified), and for the first time customers could also opt to pay an extra £39.78 for an option pack which included an outside door mirror, a swivelling map-reading lamp, a centre armrest between the seats and head restraints on the seats themselves. I have never seen records which tell how many of these packs were actually sold.

Only days after the Spitfire 1500 was announced, British Leyland ran to the British government, asking for massive financial help, and early in 1975 the Corporation was effectively nationalized. Any more improvements which *might* have been planned for the Spitfire were therefore shelved whilst yet another period of navel contemplation went ahead. In the end, the state-owned group decided that it could never make enough money from sports cars (in fact it could not make money from *any* cars for years...) and the Spitfire, like the MG Midget 1500, was left severely alone, to carry on selling in its 'as launched' configuration.

Even though independent testers clearly liked the new 1500 (*Autocar* described it as: '...a very civilised little sports car. It provides a lot of fun and has a high safety factor. The Spitfire 1500 has a lot to offer which no other car quite matches...'), Triumph was not allowed to carry on developing the design. In the next few years BL's bosses neglected not only the Spitfire, but also the Stag, the MG Midget and the MGB, and at the same time they badly mismanaged the potential of the TR7 and TR8 models.

The Spitfire, at least, took six years (and more than 90,000 examples) to die, and was one of the very last cars to be built in the Canley assembly hall. A late plan to transfer Spitfire assembly to the nearby Rover plant at Solihull was abandoned.

During those six years the 1500 was only treated to one significant freshening exercise. Starting in March 1977 (at which time a new Commission Number sequence, beginning at 100001, was initiated), the old Herald-type column switchgear was ditched in favour of TR7-type switches, there was a relocated steering column lock/ignition switch, and snazzy hound's-tooth-style seat coverings were adopted; at that juncture the UK retail price was £2,359 (£2,427 with the hardtop), which shows how rapidly British inflation was cantering ahead at that time. Except that the wheel rim width

By 1977 the USA-market Spitfire 1500 had been obliged to use large energy-absorbing rubber bumper/overriders at front and rear, which added nothing to the looks, though it kept the legislators happy.

was increased from 4.5in to 5in for the 1979 model year (from Commission No 130001), there were no further significant improvements.

Even though prices continued to soar as the £/$ exchange rate moved stubbornly against the UK in the late-1970s, the Spitfire continued to sell well in its final years. Annual production actually rose from 15,591 in 1975 to 21,189 in 1978 before the final slump began. Only 10,276 cars were built in 1979, and a mere 7,456 in 1980. The last quoted Spitfire UK price (autumn 1980) was £4,524 (£4,697 for the hardtop).

The end came in August 1980, when the last Spitfire rolled off the assembly line at Canley. A few months later the last of the Dolomite saloons was built there, after which the lines were torn up and the vast building was put to other uses.

USA 1500s – a nine-year career
As I have already explained, the first USA-market Spitfire 1500s were officially badged as Mk IVs, but all cars for all markets were badged as 1500s for 1975 and beyond. This means that the Spitfire 1500 had a nine-year career in North America, during which it sold very well indeed:

Year	Cars sold
1973	7,796
1974	7,373
1975	8,857
1976	6,846
1977	9,463
1978	10,231
1979	8,344
1980	4,037
1981	3,924★
Total	66,871

★Cars sold in 1981, of course, were 'left-overs' from cars actually built before August 1980.

The last Spitfire was built in the summer of 1980 – a right-hand-drive hardtop probably destined for delivery to a British customer.

What might have been... If this 1.85-litre overhead-cam Triumph Dolomite engine had ever been offered in the Spitfire, the result would surely have been a very attractive car with a lot more performance than the 1500 ever had. Ah well...

As in Europe, Spitfire prices were badly affected by inflation, for the 1973-model 1500 had been priced at $2,995, whereas the 1981 left-over cars sold for $6,250. It was all a far cry from the original 1963-model Spitfire, which had sold for $2,199.

Even though various safety and exhaust emission laws pressed ever harder against the Spitfire at this time, its reputation stood up very well indeed. For Triumph's engineers the only consolation was that other manufacturers had to face up to the same problems.

Along the way the US-spec car's unladen weight soared from 1,710lb to 1,875lb, the engine had to be loaded with ever more clean-up gear (a catalyst was standardized for 1977 and beyond), and for 1979 and 1980 the car was inflicted with energy-absorbing bumpers, which did nothing for the style and increased the overall length to 13ft 1.5in.

For 1980, regulations special to California were quite impossible for Triumph to meet, so the Spitfire was withdrawn from sale in that market, the largest single outlet in the USA. Sales halved in 1980, which signalled the beginning of the end, and the last Spitfires of all were not sold off in the USA until the summer of 1981.

CHAPTER 4

Spitfire in motorsport

Racing and rallying

When the Spitfire went into production, it was never intended to be used in motorsport, yet two years later there were two sets of works cars in existence. Two years after that the Spitfires had shone at Le Mans, Sebring, the Tour de France and the Alpine rally. Easy? Not at all!

As far as motorsport was concerned, Triumph realized that the original Spitfire production car was too heavy, and that the engine wasn't very tunable. But by 1964 the engine had been completely redeveloped, aluminium and glassfibre had taken the place of iron and steel all over the place, the body was more streamlined and top speeds of around 130mph were possible.

This was a project that was always dear to my heart, for as competitions secretary I was closely involved in Spitfire development. Accordingly, I hope you will excuse a personal reflection in this chapter!

Even though turning the Spitfire into a competitive car was not easy, we knew that the pundits expected nothing less; Standard-Triumph already had a fine reputation in motorsport, so the Spitfire had to match up to this. Previous works cars had chalked up major international successes in racing and rallying.

The miracle was that it had all been achieved in such a short time, mostly with near-standard cars. In 1953 there was no works team, but within five years Standard-Triumph had become one of Europe's most successful teams. When the time came to develop the Spitfire, success was expected…

The story really began in 1962. Ken Richardson's works team had been closed down in 1961, the mechanics were dispersed, the TR3As and the Le Mans TRSs had been sold off, and Standard-Triumph's new owners (Leyland) shrugged off motorsport as an expensive irrelevance.

Months later there was a change of mind. Harry Webster decided to take personal charge of a limited motorsport programme, the budget would be very small, and because I was already working at Standard-Triumph (although involved in works rallying with the Rootes team) I was asked to administer it.

In 1962 and 1963 the new works team used TR4s and Vitesses, but only in rallies. Although Harry Webster dearly wanted to get back into motor racing, that ambition would have to wait. In those two years the main innovation was for Triumph to read the Appendix J rulebook for the first time, to modify the cars to the limit of the regulations (something which Ken Richardson's team had never done), and to discover the reserves of enthusiasm in the engineering team.

In the autumn of 1963, though, there were big decisions to be made. The TR4s were struggling to stay on terms with the Porsches and Big Healeys, and the Vitesses had already been abandoned. What should be done for 1964 and beyond?

My presentation to Harry Webster pointed out that the first 'homologation specials' – the BMC Mini-Cooper S, the Ford Lotus-Cortina and the Alfa Romeo Giulia TI Super – had arrived, the Austin-Healey 3000 was beyond our reach, and special-stage rallying was progressively using rougher surfaces. We had to consider these options:

a) Pull out of motorsport altogether.

b) Carry on with increasingly uncompetitive TR4s.
c) Develop new cars, some specifically for racing/tarmac rallying, and some for rough-road rallying. This would cost a lot of money.

I knew that the company was longing to go back to Le Mans, so for option (c) I suggested that the tarmac cars should be Spitfires and the rough-road cars should be 2000s.

If Harry Webster had been a finance man, a 'number cruncher', he would have admitted that 1960s motorsport was getting expensive, and walked away from it altogether. But Harry was a motoring enthusiast, a capable engineer, and he well knew what successful motorsport could do for the company's image. There was little hesitation from him, or from his fellow directors, and a serious development programme was agreed.

For 1964, therefore, it was decided that three sets of new cars should be developed:

A set of Triumph 2000s for rough-road rallying.
A set of homologated Spitfires for tarmac rallying.
A set of lightweight prototype Spitfires for the Le Mans 24-hour race.

Furthermore, my department would look after the rallying programme, but the Le Mans cars would be developed in the engineering department. Because the Le Mans date clashed with the Alpine rally, this made sense; the result was that workshop manager John Lloyd looked after the Le Mans programme, the cars actually taking shape within 10 yards of his office door, while Ray Henderson ran the rally shop.

Design work began in October 1963 (board approval only came in December 1963 – Harry Webster was like that!), with several targets to be met. Two race cars had to be ready for the Le Mans test weekend in April 1964, four race cars had to be ready for Le Mans itself in June 1964, and four rally cars had to be ready for the Alpine rally, which started immediately after Le Mans finished.

To turn the Spitfire into a car which should become a class winner, my department combed the rulebook to see what modifications could legally be made. We also gave a lot of

thought to those details which we thought we could get away with, but that's another story...

Work concentrated on four areas – getting a lot more power out of the engine, getting weight out of the car, improving the roadholding, and (specifically for Le Mans) improving the shape.

Engine and transmission modifications

For the car to be competitive, the team knew that more than 100bhp would be needed from the 1,147cc engine, but that the standard unit was quite incapable of this. All earlier attempts by independent tuners to make a Herald engine into a front-running Formula Junior unit had failed miserably. Its existing cylinder-head, with siamesed inlet ports, was altogether too asthmatic.

This was the start of the Spitfire rallying programme. The date is April 1964, four brand-new powder-blue Spitfires have just been stripped, and careful assembly for motorsport has begun. Anyone who gets excited about car identities should realize that this process, and a lot of 'mix-and-match', occurred after every event.

On the Spitfire's first rally – the 1964 French Alpine – Terry Hunter and Patrick Lier brought ADU 7B to within one minute of an Alpine *Coupe*. It was the only occasion on which Triumph works rally cars were used in 'bubble-top' form.

Fortunately, the engine designers, led by Ray Bates, knew this and were already working on prototype eight-port cylinder-heads for the forthcoming Triumph 1300 front-wheel-drive saloon. This layout, which was fundamentally redeveloped in the next few months, was the linchpin of the '70X' competition engine's layout.

Together with the use of large twin-choke Weber carburettors, a free-flow exhaust manifold, ambitious camshaft timing and a great deal of work on cylinder-head breathing, crankshaft and bearing specifications and the baffling of the sump, the target power was achieved. So that the works cylinder-heads could use the largest possible valves, tiny 10mm motorcycle-type sparking plugs were used; in certain conditions this made the engines very difficult to start from cold.

In 1964 there were, in fact, two entirely different types of eight-port cylinder-head for competition use (and the homologation authorities never noticed...), one being made of cast iron, the other of cast aluminium. The cast-iron head was thought to give better prospects of reliability; the Le Mans cars used it, with a peak rating of 98bhp at 6,750rpm. The use of an aluminium head was thought to be a gamble at first, but the rally car engines were always fitted with such components, where peak power was 102.5bhp at 7,000rpm.

In retrospect, it seems that the Webers were too large for their task, and the gas flow was still not good enough (Triumph was too proud to consult Cosworth, who might have made different recommendations), but although the engines always used a lot of fuel and had very little low-speed torque, they eventually became fairly reliable.

For 1964, the race cars (being prototypes) were fitted with TR4-type all-synchromesh gearboxes, while the first rally cars were fitted with the homologated close-ratio (Vitesse-type) gearboxes, which did not have bottom-gear synchromesh. Rear axles of prototype GT6 types were fitted (with newly developed Salisbury limited-slip differentials), these being visually similar to existing Spitfire types.

Chassis, suspension and brakes
Except for the engines, the cars' completed rolling chassis looked surprisingly standard. Initial proposals to lighten the

cars by using modified chassis-frames were abandoned after tests showed up a loss of rigidity; in fact, reinforcement was added in several areas, particularly for rally car use.

To improve the roadholding the cars were fitted with wider-rim wheels (4.5in instead of 3.5in) – cast aluminium for race cars, Courier van-type for rally cars – and endless tests at MIRA showed that the cars could be made to handle very well indeed if springs, dampers and, above all, camber angles could be carefully respecified.

Various specialists offered their wares, notably the auxiliary rear springs which limited camber change, but the conclusion that the best compromise was to use hard springs, firm dampers, negative-camber rear wheels and the best possible Dunlop tyres, was accepted happily by all the drivers. The cars' performance on road and track, backed up by all the pictures, confirmed this to be right.

The weight distribution/roadholding balance was compromised by the decision to use vast 18-gallon aluminium fuel tanks above the rear axle of the race cars, the difference between full and empty being 144lb/65kg!

Brakes were enlarged where possible – larger front discs and calipers were matched on the homologated rally cars by 8in rear drums, the race cars having TR4-type 9in rear drums instead.

Bodies – shape and weight
In the beginning, the race car and rally car bodies were very different indeed. The rally cars had to run in homologated specification, while the prototype race cars could include any change which made them more efficient.

The prototype race cars had basic bodies which were made almost completely from aluminium panels, which had been produced on the production press tools. In addition, they were given glassfibre fastback hardtops which were actually moulded straight off the Spitfire GT development car's shell. (Note, therefore, that what became the GT6 roof was actually in existence before the Le Mans project took shape, not the other way round, as one might assume.)

The cars ran at the Le Mans test days in April 1964 with normally shaped bonnets, but for the race itself these were reshaped to have faired-in headlamps and a much-reduced

For the Tour de France in September 1964, three rally cars were considerably modified, having their own version of the Le Mans/GT6-style fastback in glassfibre while at the same time three Le Mans bonnets were borrowed and resprayed for the occasion. ADU 7B won its class and demolished all opposition from the Alpine-Renault works cars.

radiator grille aperture.

Because the rules surrounding homologation only allowed the material of skin panels to be changed, the rally cars used basically standard shells with alumnium skins. For their first event, the 1964 Alpine rally, they were fitted with conventional removable hardtops, and ran with standard 8.25-gallon fuel tanks.

Both sets of cars had air outlet grilles in the sides of the bonnet assemblies, but neither was ever tested in a wind-tunnel. Bumpers were not fitted to race cars, but had to be retained on rally cars.

To get the show on the road as soon as possible in 1964, the works team took charge of 412 VC, which was an original 1962 Spitfire development car, and steadily developed it in several British events, with Roy Fidler as the driver. Its best result was second overall in the Welsh International rally, but as a mobile test-bed it was an invaluable tool.

Race cars – 1964 to 1966
Until the middle of 1964, the biggest development worry was over the reliability of engines. Several units expired on the test-beds because of piston or crankshaft bearing failures, and an Oulton Park test run was stopped after 65 laps, but the Le Mans test weekend was successful, and by June the crossed fingers were not quite as firmly in place.

Four new cars, registered ADU 1B, ADU 2B, ADU 3B and ADU 4B, were built up in 1964, each carrying an experimental Commission Number. Each was painted British Racing Green, with a variety of individual nose flashing so that the pit crews could pick one from another.

Although only two firm entries were assured at Le Mans in June 1964, all four cars were transported to the circuit, and a third car was allowed to start after the qualifying sessions; ADU 4B was the car which sat, unused, during the weekend. At scrutineering the cars weighed between 1,625lb and 1,640lb.

During the race all three cars proved capable of lapping in about 4min 55sec, recording top speeds of 134mph (using a 3.89:1 rear axle and more than 7,000rpm...), but crashes eliminated two of them. The survivor (driven by David

The startline of yet another race in the Tour de France features the Slotemaker/Hunter Spitfire on the front row of the grid alongside the works MG MGB and one of the factory-backed Alpine-Renaults. The Thuner/Gretener Spitfire is on the second row.

On their first public appearance, two racing Spitfires appeared at the Le Mans 24 Hours race test day in April 1964. At this stage they still had conventionally shaped bonnets, and there was still more power to come from the engines.

ADU 3B at Le Mans in 1964, when it was driven by Jean-Louis Marnat and Jean-François Piot. Note the streamlined 'E-type' bonnet style, the blanked off front grille and the 'Team Triumph' badges on the flanks.

58

This was the engine bay of a 1964 works racing Spitfire, complete with twin dual-choke Weber carburettors. An oil cooler, invisible in this view, was mounted ahead of the water radiator.

Hobbs and Rob Slotemaker) finished strongly in 21st place, averaging 94.7mph including all stops and recording 22.4mpg. It was third in its class behind two very special Alpine-Renaults, but it beat the works Austin-Healey Sprite by no less than 124 miles.

There was no other works team effort in 1964, but for 1965 two new cars were built up to replace the two wrecked machines (but they carried the same identities). For the Sebring 12-hour race in Florida, in March, three of the cars were entered as homologated machines (which meant gearbox and brake changes from 1964, but somehow the aluminium/glassfibre shells were retained, and passed by the scrutineers). Two cars finished second and third in their class. Once again it was the original car, ADU 1B, which was crashed, but it was rebuilt in time for the Le Mans race in June 1965.

All four cars were sent to Le Mans in 1965, and this time all four started the race. As at Sebring they ran as homologated GT cars, yet they were fitted with thin-gauge chassis-frames, which saved 31lb. This, plus the use of

The 1965 Sebring line-up of the three Spitfires, all of which ran in the GT category, even though all-aluminium bodies were used. Car No 25, at the rear, is actually a Jaguar E-Type – the bonnet shape resemblance is clear!

Peter Bolton in ADU 1B at Sebring in 1965. Crashed and written off at Le Mans in 1964, it had been recreated during the winter, only for Bolton to roll it again later in this race...

Bob Tullius was Triumph-USA's young star driver in the early 1960s so he drove the Spitfire race cars on several occasions. His partner, Charlie Gates, is at the wheel of their Sebring car, ADU 2B, at this moment.

Final preparations for a Spitfire race car. Ray Henderson, wielding a cloth, is at the front wheel, engine tuner Dennis Barbet is leaning into the engine bay, while mechanic Roger Sykes is by the driver's door.

One of the 1965 Spitfires at Le Mans, at pit-stop time, showing that aluminium shields had been built along each side of the engine bay so that the Weber carburettors could gulp cold air. Note that only one wiper blade is fitted. Spitfires finished first and second in their class on this occasion.

prototype GT6-type gearboxes and aluminium cylinder-heads, meant they weighed only 1,520lb.

This time their engines produced 109bhp, and their top speed was about 140mph, this being a real advance over the first year's performance. It was an extremely successful outing. Two cars finished first and second in their capacity class, one crashed at White House, while the fourth retired when engine oil leaked from a split oil-cooler. ADU 4B, driven by Jean-Jacques Thuner and Simo Lampinen, averaged 95.1mph and took 13th place overall.

Although that was the end of the Spitfire's official works career, there are several footnotes. From time to time, race or rally cars (or merely engines and transmissions from one of the cars) were lent out to private entrants, but there were no other official team entries.

In 1965, a fifth works-type car (ERW 412C) was built up for Bill Bradley to race in European sports car events, this car (and its successor, the much-modified ADU 2B) winning many classes in its career.

Later in 1965, too, Walter Sulke, the Standard-Triumph

The Quaker State oil company backed Bob Tullius' Group 44 team for several successful years in USA racing. This was Brian Furstenau's well-known Spitfire Mk 3, which won many races in SCCA Class F Production events in the late 1960s.

The unmistakable profile of a works Le Mans Spitfire racing car, showing its GT6-style glassfibre hardtop, its streamlined nose (which Triumph copied from the Jaguar E-Type), and the functional air outlets in the sides of the bonnet. All the cars had brackets, front and rear, for quick-lift jacks to be used.

The very special Spitfire being built-up for export to Hong Kong in 1965 so that Walter Sulke could race it in the Far East. Based on the Spitfire racing cars, it has a special 'E-type' headrest and a wrap-round windscreen.

Another detail view of the Macau car, showing the wrap-round screen, the stripped-out interior, the leather-trimmed steering wheel and the very simple instrument panel. It was a *very* light car – note the way in which the doors have been gutted.

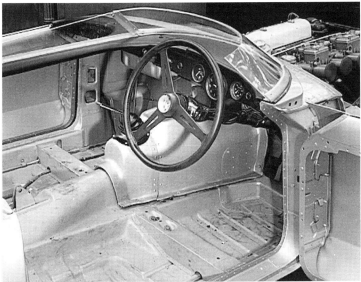

importer in Hong Kong, persuaded the factory to build up a sprint version from spare parts, which was effectively the sixth car. The result was a very attractive open-top version, with a head fairing and a 'single-seater' perspex cowl around the driver's seat. Any resemblance to the Jaguar D-type was strictly intentional! This car won several events in the Pacific region, but never raced in Europe.

Incidentally, for 1966 the factory considered building a set of GT6-based cars, to be called GT6R (R=Racing, I suppose), but the single prototype was cancelled when half-built.

Rally cars – 1964 and 1965
Once the lessons of 412 VC had been digested, four brand new works cars, painted powder blue and registered ADU 5B, ADU 6B, ADU 7B and ADU 8B, were prepared in the early months of 1964. There was also a fifth semi-works car for Valerie Pirie and the Stirling Moss Automobile Racing Team to use; this car was painted a special green colour and registered ADU 467B.

The Macau Spitfire in all its glory, ready for shipment. In later life this car found its way to the USA, where apparently a GT6 engine was fitted. A complete replica of this car is being built by Bernard Robinson of the Triumph Sports Six Club.

Their finest hour. The 1965 Le Mans race, where Spitfires were first and second in their class, the faster of the cars averaging 95.1mph. This particular car – ADU 2B – retired with a blown engine when the oil-cooler split.

In 1964 and 1965 Triumph also maintained this works replica Spitfire for Valerie Pirie and the Stirling Moss Automobile Racing Team. To take advantage of new-type quartz-halogen headlamp bulbs (which only had a single filament at this time), an extra pair of secondary dipping lamps was fitted into the bonnet of the cars in 1965.

For their first event (the Alpine rally) ADU 5B, 6B, 7B and 467B were all equipped with standard hardtops and bonnets and ran with aluminium heads and Vitesse 1600 gear ratios. After two crashes and one engine failure, only one car (that of Terry Hunter) finished, missing its *Coupe des Alpes* by one minute (and that was the fault of team management, which held it back too long at one service point), but taking third in its class.

Before the Tour de France, which took place less than three months later, the cars were extensively re-engineered, for they were given prototype GT6 all-synchromesh gearboxes, the 18-gallon Le Mans fuel tanks and modified

versions of the Le Mans-type glassfibre fastback roof panels. For these cars, however, there was a rectangular bootlid on the tail to allow the spare wheel to be removed; Valerie Pirie's car was never converted.

For the Tour de France, cast-iron cylinder-heads were used, and the bonnets of the Le Mans cars were borrowed. Once again, three cars retired, all with engine failure, but the Slotemaker/Hunter car not only won its class, but finished 10th overall in the GT category (behind, among other cars, four Ferrari GT0s and four Porsche 904s!). The Spitfires beat every French Alpine-Renault or Bonnet, which worked wonders for the car's image in France.

Daylight, and the end of the difficult night section of the 1965 Monte Carlo rally. One of the Spitfires is clocked in at Pont Charles Albert, just north of Nice.

A few weeks later, the French pair, Piot and Marnat, used ADU 5B to win their class in the Paris 1,000km race, while Terry Hunter and Jean-Jacques Thuner finished second and fifth overall in the Geneva rally, and first and second in their class, and helped Triumph to win the team prize.

In 1965, the cars were all given neatly styled extra inboard-mounted headlamp pods, Simo Lampinen joined the team, and a new left-hand-drive car (AVC 654B) was built for him. In the Monte Carlo rally, Lampinen was 10th until the last night, when his engine blew, while Rob Slotemaker's car finished second in its class.

Later in the year, Thuner took fifth overall in the Geneva rally, winning his class from Simo Lampinen's sister car, while for the famous Alpine rally the cars were entered in the prototype category. For that event they were given 117bhp 1,296cc aluminium-headed engines, and produced a sensational result. Not only did Lampinen's car win its class, with Thuner's second, but the two cars won the category outright, outlasting such purpose-built racing cars as the Porsche 904s.

Withdrawal

At the end of the 1965 season, rallying's Appendix J regulations changed significantly, not only banning the use of alternative body skin panel material, but also forbidding different shapes and the use of alternative cylinder-heads. For all those reasons the works Spitfire effort was terminated at the end of the season, and the cars were either scrapped or eventually sold off.

Some have survived to this day, mostly in extremely non-standard condition. One or two near-replicas have been built in recent years (though works cylinder-heads are no longer available); the most ambitious is a Macau-car replica, by a Triumph Sports Six Club official.

CHAPTER 5

GT6 Mk 1

Six-cylinder coupe style

I should make one thing clear at the start of this chapter: there was no thought of making the GT6 when the Spitfire was conceived, nor any GT6 plan when the Spitfire was launched. The idea of building a six-cylinder version of the Spitfire only came along in 1964.

Even so, the original type of GT6 was not the car which eventually went on sale in 1966. The car we now know as the GT6, in fact, had a very complicated development history. I can sum it up by quoting three main influences – the Spitfire itself, the project once called the Spitfire GT, and the six-cylinder Vitesse.

The first step along the road to the GT6 came in 1963 when the ever-inventive Webster/Turnbull/Michelotti team decided to play around with the idea of a Spitfire GT. This, in effect, was a standard Spitfire fitted with a smart new fastback/hatchback roof, the only mechanical changes being to relocate the fuel tank and alter the rear suspension stiffness to take account of the car's extra weight.

The one and only Spitfire GT was a conversion of the prototype Spitfire – X691, registered 4305 VC – and was completed in 1963, painted bright red. It had a very glossy facia panel, in polished wood, which was completely covered in instruments and switches. The project was discussed at director level in August 1963, and again in December 1963 (when a launch date of October 1964 was discussed), but no decisions were taken.

The problem was that the 63bhp Spitfire GT looked good and was well-equipped, but was too heavy, used more petrol and was less lively than the standard version. Clearly it was not saleable in that form.

By this time, of course, the six-cylinder Vitesse had joined the four-cylinder Herald on the production lines, which meant that engineers and production staff knew all about the installation of a longer 'six' into an engine bay which had been designed to accept a 'four'. If it could be done in the saloon, surely it could also be done in the sports car?

Early in 1964, therefore, the single Spitfire GT prototype was redesigned by having a Vitesse 1600 engine and close-ratio gearbox installed, though the 4.11:1 rear axle ratio was retained. At that stage, to give clearance for the longer engine, a rather angular bonnet bulge was added, with a forward-facing intake.

I took this car to France in June 1964 (specifically to the Le Mans race circuit to see the race organizers), and on my return I recommended several changes, notably the redesign of the passenger windows (which sucked out at high speed) and the fitment of larger-section tyres, larger brakes and higher overall gearing.

The 1.6-litre car was quicker than the 1.1-litre type, but not dramatically so. In refined twin-Zenith-Stromberg carburettor form it only had 77bhp, compared with the Spitfire's 63bhp, and it struggled to reach 100mph. The sales department knew what it would have to charge for the car, and was still not impressed.

Fortunately for this project, the Vitesse model was also in some sales trouble, particularly in the USA, where it was not considered powerful enough. Also fortunately, and quite coincidentally, Standard-Triumph had become very profitable once again, and serious money was made available to improve and upgrade existing models and invest in new types. The fact that the motor industry's rumour factory had also started to mention a fastback/hatchback version of the MGB, which was to be launched in the autumn of 1965, was another important stimulus.

Accordingly, it was decided to develop two new models using the same components. The most important innovations were the use of 2-litre engines and a new-fangled all-synchromesh gearbox. There was also a considerably stronger version of the chassis-mounted rear axle, but as this was hidden away it never made any headlines.

The result, which went public in October 1966 when production had already begun, was the arrival of the Vitesse 2-litre and the launch of the GT6.

All these major changes were made without incurring any space problems, for the 2-litre engine had exactly the same bulk as the 1.6-litre unit, the new all-synchromesh gearbox was no bulkier and mere fractions of an inch longer than the

This hybrid car, affectionately known as the 'Kenilworth dragster', was originally the prototype Vitesse coupe (although such a car never went into production). It was experience with this car which led Harry Webster to propose the new GT6 coupe.

Before the GT6 went on sale, this graceful prototype by Michelotti, a 2-litre six-cylinder-engined mono-coque machine coded 'Fury', was built. Only one car was made, and it survives to this day.

This was a very early example of the GT6, UK-registered but in left-hand-drive form, showing the way that the fastback roof, and a bonnet bulge, had enhanced the original lines of the Spitfire.

old 'crash-first' type, while the final-drive was the same size as before.

Right from the start the new sports coupe was christened GT6, and its character was always developed with the North American market in mind, where most sales were expected to take place. Compared to the Spitfire, it was to be a much more refined and civilized car, with a smoother engine, a quieter exhaust system, better trim, more comprehensive equipment, and an altogether softer ride. It was, in other words, to be much more of a GT than a sports car.

Development went ahead so smoothly in 1965 and 1966 that only three prototypes were needed – X691 (which had started life as a Spitfire), X742 (registered EVC 375C) and X746 (FWK 319D). The works racing and rallying Spitfires had not only shown that the shape was very efficient – 130mph was possible with suitable gearing – but they had also proved to be very stable at high speeds. The coupe body style, therefore, was never checked out in a wind-tunnel, and there were only minor visual differences between the 1963 prototype and the 1966 production car.

These included swivelling front quarter-lights in the doors, a different grille and lights, bonnet cooling louvres and a modified shape to the bonnet bulge. The production car's bonnet appeared to have been inspired by that of Jaguar's famous E-Type, indeed the whole car had that type of stance.

The Pressed Steel Company provided the large roof/tail panel to Forward Radiator, which assembled the shell on modified versions of Spitfire body tooling. Inside the cabin, which was the same width as that of the Spitfire, but considerably longer, there was a long wooden-floored loading space behind the sumptuously trimmed front seats, and the hatchback lifted up (the same as that of the MGB GT, rather

Original-type GT6s had this rather fussily detailed rear quarter, complete with three separate Lucas lights, quarter-bumpers and a snap-action petrol filler cap. Note, too, the wire wheels with which many GT6s were fitted.

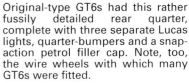

The number-plate tells its own story, but it isn't only for display. This already personalized example is carrying Le Mans success stickers in the rear window.

This is a well-known picture, but it shows just how snugly the long Standard-Triumph six-cylinder engine fitted into the engine compartment of the GT6. The carburettor air cleaners, for example, are overhanging the splash-guards at the side of the engine bay. This engine has Zenith-Stromberg carburettors.

than sideways as on the Jaguar E-Type), aided in its action by torsion bars fixed to the concealed hinges. The factory claimed no less than 14.2cu ft of stowage space, almost all of this being exposed to view from above. The rear quarter-windows could be cracked open to help through-flow ventilation.

The polished walnut facia had a new arrangement of instruments and switches – different from existing Spitfires, and different again from that of the original Spitfire GT –

with switchgear and controls lifted from the new Triumph 1300 saloon. For the first time on this sports car family, the speedometer and rev-counter were ahead of the driver's eyes. There was a parcel shelf ahead of the passenger, and a large padded grab handle.

Pedals and steering column controls were exactly as used in the Spitfire, though there was a smaller leather-padded steering wheel, 15in in diameter. The floor was completely carpeted, and the doors were padded with carpet kick-strips.

There was an armrest between the seats, from which the handbrake lever sprouted.

The seats, in particular, looked inviting, even though they were quite small, as they were sensibly shaped, with squashy rolls under the thighs and well-padded supports along their sides.

For every enthusiast, however, the GT6 hid all its important novelties – engine, gearbox, back axle and brakes – out of sight. All appeared to have been packaged without difficulty, though the engine itself was much longer than that of the Spitfire and had forced a squat radiator to be positioned at the front extremity of the under-bonnet space.

Except that it was repositioned in an upright position, the new 2-litre engine was virtually the same as that of the modern Triumph 2000 saloon, where it was canted over at 10 degrees for installation reasons. With a 9.5:1 compression ratio (which, incidentally, meant that Triumph recommended that 5-star, 100-octane fuel should be used, which was easy in 1966, but impossible today) and twin Zenith-Stromberg carburettors, it was rated at 95bhp. There was only a slim air-cleaner box for the carburettors, which actually overhung the right-side splash-guard to the engine bay.

The gearbox was a newly developed four-speed close-ratio all-synchromesh unit, which (as already recounted in Chapter 4) had been used in competition Spitfires since 1964, one which would one day be used in Dolomite saloon cars and (in wide-ratio form) in later models of the Spitfire. As with the Spitfire, Laycock overdrive was optional, and operated on top and third gears.

The final-drive was much more robust than before. Customer complaints of problems with the Spitfires and Vitesses, plus motorsport experience, had inspired a redesign of the assembly so that it could withstand higher snatch loads. On non-overdrive cars the ratio was 3.27:1, while overdrive-equipped cars had the 3.89:1 ratio first used on the racing Spitfires.

To match all this, 4.5in width wheel rims were standardized (disc wheels or centre-lock wire wheels being available to choice), bigger front discs and calipers and 8in rear brake drums were specified, while 155–13in radial-ply tyres were also used. The actual brake swept area was up from 199sq in on the Spitfire to 260sq in on the GT6.

The two items which caused most of the grumbles from the press when the car was launched concerned the steering and handling. To take account of the extra front-end weight (1,127lb compared with 910lb for the original Spitfire) and to keep steering efforts low, the steering ratio was dropped, and for the GT6 there were no fewer than 4.25 steering wheel turns from lock to lock.

Even though the GT6 appeared four full years (and a lot of press criticism) into the career of the Spitfire, there had been no attempt to get rid of the obvious faults of the high-pivot swing-axle rear suspension, and when the front wheels were over in the full-lock position there was a great deal of tyre scrub.

Although the suspension itself and its geometry were the same as for the Spitfire, the GT6 felt to be a considerably softer car. As I commented when I wrote the original new-car launch material for *Autocar*: 'The rack and pinion steering is low geared so quite a lot of wheel twirling is needed to hustle the little car around twisting lanes. Damper settings are definitely softer than those of the Spitfire, no doubt to provide a "boulevard" ride favoured by the Americans.'

The new GT6 went on sale in the UK at a price of £985, which is worth comparing with the price of a Spitfire (with hardtop), which cost £712. To put the car even further into perspective, the MGB GT was selling for £1,016, the TR4A with hardtop for £1,028, and the 1.6-litre Sunbeam Alpine GT for £954.

In those days, however, customers were still expected to dig deeper into their pockets to get what we would call today a fully equipped car. On top of the £985 price, safety belts cost £8, the optional overdrive £58, wire-spoke wheels £37 and the heater £13.50.

The GT6 appealed strongly to some, and not to others. Its major advantages – styling, equipment, practicality and refinement – were somewhat offset by its small cabin, its too-soft character, its wayward handling and its high price. In later years I even heard it described, very unkindly, as 'the answer to a question which was never actually posed!'.

Motor, for sure, called it: '"A businessman's express" for the less-affluent businessman', but on the other hand there

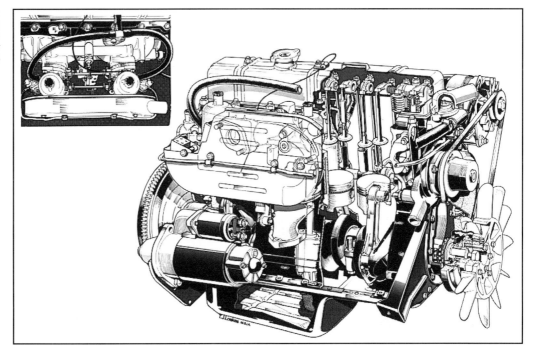

Although this engine drawing is of a 2.5-litre example, with a long-stroke crankshaft, it shows off the architecture of all the six-cylinder engines used in the building of GT6 sports coupes.

was the comment: 'On a racing circuit the limitations of a simple swing axle, set up for touring use, are more evident and "nosing in" is very pronounced – on a wet road it might be embarrassing. We spent most of the time on the 180deg south curve at Mallory Park hovering between power-on and power-off in search of a neutral and predictable line.' Even so, in another issue the GT6 was described as: 'Altogether an entertaining car and one of the fastest you can buy for £1,000.'

For Triumph, the important question was how the enthusiasts would react, and to get a feel for this they must have been anxious to see what magazines like Britain's *Autosport* or North America's *Road & Track* had to say.

As usual, John Bolster of *Autosport* was happy to try a new model and to transmit his enthusiasms. He started by musing on the merits of large engines in small cars before going on to

discuss the layout. He was not completely complimentary about the cabin or its equipment, pointing out that 'the body is by no means cramped, though the low roof gives a rather beetle-browed effect'. He also worried about stowage in the tail, under clear glass, wishing that 'some sort of cover might be arranged to conceal these from miscreants, who think nothing of smashing a window nowadays...'.

Clearly, too, JVB liked the handling: 'The ride is firm and very little roll is apparent...Though the GT6 is naturally heavier in front than the Spitfire it is a well-balanced car, and the tail may be hung out under suitable circumstances. Tested on a racing circuit in wet and slippery conditions, the car gave plenty of confidence and returned good lap times.'

That report was certainly encouraging, and *Road & Track* was no less impressed: 'We liked the 2-litre six in the 2000 and we like it even better in the GT6...It's nice to have an

The original Spitfire GT of 1963 had this interior, which was only lightly modified when the GT became a GT6 shortly afterwards.

engine with enough torque that you don't have to operate the gearbox constantly.'

Not only that, but the testers liked the chassis: 'We approach any car with conventional swing axles with a little apprehension, but we found that the GT6 could not be faulted on its handling...For ordinary-to-brisk driving, the car steers neutrally and simply goes where it's steered with great apparent stability. The tail can be brought out at will either by poking the throttle (in the right gear, naturally) or by just tweaking the wheel a little too much. Breakaway is smooth

and one gets the feeling that the car has a degree of oversteer that can be enjoyed and utilized by a moderately skilled driver while never crossing up an unskilled one.'

Not only that, but *Road & Track* summarized as follows: 'It's a great improvement over the Spitfire 4 from which it descended. Not that the Spitfire 4 was bad, it's just that the GT6 is so much better. It has no parallel and it's worth the money.'

Fortunately for Triumph, the dealers could begin to satisfy sales demand almost as soon as the GT6 was revealed. The

The GT6 Mk 1 at its first London motor show. Fitted with optional wire-spoke wheels and whitewall Goodyear tyres, it would become a familiar sight on British and American roads during the next few months.

This was the original shape of the GT6. It is instructive to compare it with the racing Spitfires illustrated in the previous chapter.

first few off-tools examples were built in July and August 1966, but a further 120 cars were assembled in September. Then the trickle turned into a flood – 149 cars were built in October, 276 in November, 504 in December and 673 in January 1967, before production settled down to between 500 and 600 a month.

In North America, deliveries began at the end of 1966, when the GT6 was priced at $3,039. Centre-lock wire wheels and Dunlop SP41 radial-ply tyres were standard, while overdrive was a $175 extra. In the USA (as in the home market) Triumph's important achievement was to make the GT6 marginally cheaper than the rival MGB GT, and the result was that within a year the GT6 was matching the MGB GT, sale for sale.

Within that first year, too, the GT6 had achieved a controversial reputation. No-one interested in buying a car of that size or character had the same opinions nor, it seemed, the same standards or requirements. There were widely different opinions of its handling, of its styling, and of its small cabin.

Even so, the GT6 soon became a success by any marketing or financial standards, and Standard-Triumph was delighted to see such a limited-investment car selling so strongly. The peak production month – 755 cars – came in May 1967; for comparison, in that month, 1,037 Spitfires and 448 TR4As were built. Thereafter, GT6 assembly fluctuated gently between 500 and 600 every month, and management was delighted.

Some people, for sure, misunderstood the GT6 and never came to terms with its character. It was not meant to be a sporting carry-all like the Scimitar GTE, and it was certainly not meant to be an out-and-out sports car like the TR5. For people who were in the market for a Spitfire-*sized* car, it offered a complete alternative – it was smooth where the Spitfire was sporty, high-geared where the Spitfire was a bit frantic, warm and comfortable where a Spitfire was a bit bright and breezy, and slinky where the Spitfire was a bit extrovert.

By 1967, however, criticism of the Spitfire/GT6 family's rear suspension behaviour was mounting up and, as ever, the vocal critics were very vocal indeed. Even though both cars continued to sell very well (up to 2,000 units in a good month), and though there was very little pressure for change from North America, where most of the cars were being sold, the engineers decided to make improvements.

The result, unveiled in October 1968, was the GT6 Mk 2.

CHAPTER 6

GT6 Mk 2 and Mk 3

Improving the type

When Harry Webster's engineers settled down to produce a GT6 Mk 2, they had several objectives. In particular, they wanted to produce a car with better roadholding, and they wanted to improve the ventilation inside the cabin. The fact that a more powerful engine (based on the TR5 design) also came along was merely a happy bonus.

On more than one occasion in the last 20 years, Harry Webster has reminded me that the GT6 was an immediate sales success, and that there was no overwhelming pressure from the sales force for him to make the changes. Criticism of the Vitesse 2-litre was much more pointed. When the time was ripe, some of the pressure for change actually came from him and his senior colleagues.

Harry, in fact, was an avid reader of magazines and press clippings, could see the way that the 'chattering classes' had begun to point their comments at the GT6 *and the Vitesse 2-litre*, and was determined to kill the criticisms at a stroke. It was the handling, and the oversteering characteristics, which was causing most comment – and his team soon developed an efficient 'fix' for this.

In fact, as Standard-Triumph had proved with the works competition Spitfires, there was no great difficulty in making these cars handle extremely well, even under extreme cornering forces. This, however, depended on having very precise control of static camber settings, and making spring and damper settings much firmer than those of the road cars. Neither was practical, nor acceptable, for cars built in relatively large quantities.

There was no question of tackling the GT6 on its own.

Standard-Triumph didn't have enough time, nor a surplus of engineers, for that. As in 1965, therefore, when the GT6 and Vitesse 2-litre development programmes had been carried out together, the Mk 2 programmes were dovetailed.

The engineers were hemmed in on all sides when they set out to solve the rear suspension problem. The solution was to get rid of the large changes of wheel camber which were present in the original set-up, and to this end the suspension geometry had to be changed.

For many obvious reasons – component commonality and finance being the most important – there was no question of making major changes to the chassis-frame, the bodyshell, the rear axle *or* to the general layout of the rear suspension itself when this was achieved. Whatever was to be done had to work in the same basic space envelope as before, and should be equally applicable to the Vitesse as to the GT6.

Working on the well-known basis that difficult things can be tackled at once, but the impossible takes a little time, what was eventually adopted was actually the second 'bright idea' to come from the chassis design department. The original fix, which was finally adopted for the Spitfire Mk 4, was the swing-spring mounting of the transverse leaf spring – this has already been described in Chapter 3.

For the six-cylinder cars, however, a very clever transformation was made which kept the original transverse leaf spring in place, but effectively changed the layout from high-pivot swing-axle to a double-wishbone system. The inspiration for this layout came from the Cooper Formula 1 car of the late 1950s, which also used a transverse leaf spring.

When the time came to facelift the Spitfire and GT6 models, Triumph stylists wanted to use this type of nose, with flip-up headlamps. It was a very neat proposal, but it was turned down because the directors were wary of forthcoming USA legislation which might have outlawed such lamps. The date was February 1968 – note the 'Leyland' badge on the bonnet...

On the Cooper this was by no means perfect (an upper wishbone was added to duplicate the leaf spring for the 1959 World Championship-winning season) but it was effective. Experience showed that it was no less effective on the Triumph chassis.

The new suspension geometry, in which the camber change from bump to rebound was cut dramatically from a horrifying 21deg to a much more acceptable 7deg 20min, was achieved like this:

The transverse leaf spring stayed in place, the outer sections really acting as a rather flexible upper wishbone.

A new reversed lower wishbone was fitted between the bottom of the rear wheel upright and a bracket on the chassis-frame.

A new type of drive-shaft, complete with rubber doughnut joint towards the outer end, was fitted. The doughnut was like that fitted to the front suspension of the front-drive Triumph 1300 saloon, not only cushioning the drive against torsional shocks, but allowing a degree of angular articulation at the same time. To idealize the new geometry, the forward-facing radius-arms were angled more steeply in towards the centre of the car.

Other details included the fact that the rear spring was 15% stiffer than before, and that the height of the roll-centre (which governs the ease with which the chassis tilts under side load) had been reduced from 12.8in to 6.3in.

The lower wishbone was actually a carefully shaped aluminium casting. It was bowed down to provide clearance

Compared with the original GT6, the Mk 2 had the raised bumper of the Spitfire Mk 3, extra louvres in the side of the bonnet and behind the rear quarter-windows, and those strange wheel covers (yes, the nuts are false...).

under the rubber doughnut, and was known as the reversed type because it had the single pivot at the inboard point and two pivots at the outer (wheel upright) end.

Miraculously, only three changes were needed to chassis and body structures to accommodate this new layout. New pivot brackets for the lower wishbones had to be welded on to chassis side-members, but no changes were needed to the members themselves.

On the GT6 there were relocated telescopic dampers behind the line of the drive-shafts, which were mounted to brackets on the bodyshell; on original-type cars they had been mounted to the chassis-frame itself, and on the Mk 2 Vitesse 2-litre different lever-arm dampers were used instead. New fixing positions were needed at the front end of the re-aligned radius-arms.

More power, different gearing

Even if there had been no other improvements, adding this rear suspension to the GT6 would have been enough to warrant calling it a Mark 2, but other important changes were made at the same time, which produced an altogether better car.

Mechanically, the most important improvement was to the engine, which adopted the significant changes first made to the six-cylinder unit for use in the TR5/TR250 sports cars. For that car (introduced in the autumn of 1967), and now for other six-cylinder-engined Triumphs, there was a modified cylinder block and a completely different cylinder-head casting, with more efficient breathing.

In the new GT6 application this new cylinder-head was matched to the inlet manifold of the carburetted TR250,

The GT6 Mk 2 had an even plushier facia/driving compartment than the original car, with this neat matt finish to the wooden panel. Note the face-level eyeball vents for cold air.

The backdrop is Kenilworth Castle, the date is June 1969, and the three cars on show are a GT6 Mk 2, a Spitfire Mk 3 and the then-new Triumph TR6.

along with a new high-lift/wider-overlap camshaft profile. The cylinder block, too, was the revised version first used in the TR5/TR250 models, but still in 2-litre form. The result was that peak power went up from 95bhp to 104bhp, and the engine felt to be breathing more easily. (This explains why some tuners later took the opportunity to fit 2.5-litre engines into the GT6's engine bay.)

Although there were no changes to the transmission, the engineers and the sales force juggled round with the axle-ratio/transmission combinations. For British customers, a 3.27:1 axle ratio was fitted, whether the car had overdrive or not, while 3.89:1 was relegated to the status of 'special order option'. USA cars were fitted with the previous choice of 3.27:1 without overdrive, or 3.89:1 if overdrive was specified.

In retrospect, I am sure that most people see this as a mistake. A GT6 with a 3.27:1 axle *and* overdrive was really far too high-geared, and it is significant that a high proportion of 'special order options' were placed. Significantly, the ultra-high-geared installation was abandoned when the Mk 3 was announced.

There was a further reshuffle in regard to wheels, options and markets. On the original car, of course, centre-lock wire wheels had been standard for the USA, and optional everywhere else. Now, for a revised GT6, wire-spoke wheels were to be optional extras for *all* markets, disc wheels were standard, but these were covered by what I can only describe as 'pseudo-Rostyle' covers, complete with dummy wheel nuts!

Mk 2 style and comfort

For 1969, Standard-Triumph marketed the GT6 as a GT6 Plus in North America, and as a GT6 Mk 2 in the rest of the world. Styling changes were noticeable, but radical, and the improvement in creature comforts was obvious. In the USA, GT6 prices rose for 1969 to $2,995 (a modest $100 more than in 1968), and in the UK from £1,024 to £1,148. In the UK, overdrive cost £60.70 extra and wire-spoke wheels £38.33.

Inside the car there was a new facia style, with matt wood instead of polished wood, with a TR5-type steering wheel (the wire spokes being hidden under pads), and safety-type switch gear. The most important change, however, was to provide the passengers with cool-air face-level ventilation, for there were two adjustable 'eyeball' outlets on the instrument panel.

Not only that, but the cars were henceforth to be equipped with an electrically heated rear window glass, and there were air outlet grilles (from the cabin) in the rear quarter panels, behind the quarter-window glasses).

The external changes allowed the latest GT6 to line up with the current Spitfire Mk 3, which meant that the front bumper had been raised by several inches so that it was placed squarely across, rather than under, the radiator grille opening. In addition, the bonnet cooling vents had been reinforced by additional vents, which were located behind the wheelarches and ahead of the bonnet holding-down catches. Clearly this was a truly determined attempt to clear the hot under-bonnet air to the outside world. The only changes at the rear were to the badges.

This much-revised GT6 was indeed a better car than the original type, yet surprisingly enough this made virtually no difference to sales, which suggests that GT6 customers were already quite happy with the size, type and character of the car they were being offered.

In fact, according to the latest figures supplied to me by BMIHT, 7,366 Mk 1s were produced in 1967, yet only 6,990 were produced in 1969. General export production peaked in 1968 (Mk 1 and Mk 2 models) at 6,247, dropped to 5,749 a year later, and continued to slide steadily thereafter. No, I don't understand this either...

Even so, there is no doubt that the GT6 continued to improve with every model year which passed. Like other sporting Triumphs of the period, it was never neglected by the engineers or the sales force, so that advertisers and salesmen always had something to talk about.

It was, however, a specialized little car, a rather slim two-seater (in spite of the offer of an occasional rear seat for a time), fast, refined, but not very spacious. It was so specialized, indeed, that it could correctly be described as unique.

As *Road & Track* commented in its February 1969 road test: 'Where else can you get a 6-cyl, 100+ mph coupe with a proper chassis, good finish and jazzy looks for $3,000? Nowhere *we* know of.'

For 1970 (announced in September 1969), a whole series of cosmetic improvements was made to the GT6, which accorded with those applied to the Spitfire at the same time. There were reclining seats (not that they could be reclined very far in this compact cabin), a new-style steering wheel like that of the TR6, with aluminium spokes, more cockpit

Triumph's sporting car line-up in 1972. Top to bottom are a Spitfire Mk IV, GT6 Mk 3, TR6, Stag and Dolomite 1850.

padding for safety reasons, and a matt black windscreen surround (instead of chrome). At the same time the UK price rose from £1,148 to £1,180, the USA price from $2,995 to $3,095.

GT6 Mk 3 – new clothes for the 1970s

As already described in Chapter 3, Triumph's small sports car body was completely reskinned for the 1970s. Because of this, and allied to the mechanical improvements made, the Spitfire moved up from Mk 3 to Mk IV. At the same time the GT6 moved up from Mk 2 to Mk 3. It also became simpler

to keep track of GT6 developments in the USA because at this time its title changed from GT6 Plus to GT6 Mk 3.

Because the GT6 bodyshell was based closely on that of the Spitfire, the Mk 3 picked up all the new features of the reskinned Spitfire and added some of its own. In general, therefore, it had the 'de-seamed' bonnet, complete with more delicately detailed nose and with the slimmer bumper nicely integrated into the front aperture. It had the squared-off tail, complete with a much neater stop/tail/indicator lamp arrangement, it had the recessed pull-out type of door handles and the deepened windscreen.

There was space for the GT6's engine in the bay originally intended for the four-cylinder unit, but only just. The carburettor air cleaners drew their air through cool air pipes plumbed in to the nose of the car.

The GT6 Mk 3 cockpit looked similar to that of the Mk 2, but when overdrive was fitted the switch control was now recessed into the top of the gearlever knob.

Clearly, Standard-Triumph's engineers had cured the engine bay cooling problem, for there were no longer any cooling louvres either on top of the bonnet, or on the flanks. The cabin had reshaped rear quarter-windows, and a new louvred extractor panel was placed behind it.

The fastback roof itself was reprofiled (the Mk 1 and Mk 2 cars looked slightly hump-backed, but there was no such impression with the Mk 3), and the petrol tank filler cap had been relocated from the tail to the left-side rear wing, behind and above the rear wheelarch. Last, but by no means least, new-style road wheels with exposed wheel nuts were fitted.

Inside the car, equipment changes were confined to the fitment of an ignition/steering lock on the column of British-market cars (this was about to become compulsory) and to the use of different heater controls, while the overdrive control switch was located in the gear-lever knob, like that of several other Triumph sports cars of the day.

Under this neat little skin, mechanical changes were

Rear view of the GT6 Mk 3 showing the better detailing of the tail and corners, recessed fuel filler cap in the left-side rear wing, and the large and practical opening of the hatchback lid. The cable going into the car through the left-side door is probably a lead for the photographer's spotlamp.

minimal. The engine power, for the moment, stayed at 104bhp (net) for the UK-market cars, while the choice of rear axle ratios returned to the sensible Mk 1 arrangement – 3.89:1 with overdrive, 3.27:1 without overdrive.

The fact that the GT6 Mk 3 was a better, prettier and more practical car than the Mk 2 did not seem to do anything for its sales, which continued to slip gradually downwards, whether in the USA (still a *very* important market territory) or in the UK. All the signs are that British Leyland, which had controlled the Triumph business since 1968, became

This GT6 Mk 3 has extra foglamps mounted low down and at each side of the radiator grille. This was a 1973 model, with the wider rear track. Production ended in 1973 after a seven-year run.

The Triumph Sports Six Club put this immaculate GT6 Mk 3 on show at one of their displays in the 1980s, when it was surrounded by Heralds, Vitesses and Spitfires.

reconciled to this, for little further development work was done on the car during the next three years, and production ended in 1973.

Apart from the fact that sales stuck stubbornly below the 6,000 per year level, there were two main reasons for this. One was that a great deal of effort had to go into keeping the engine abreast of exhaust emission regulations in the USA and in the UK, the second that ever more so-called safety features had to be engineered, tested and fitted to North American-market machines. Inevitably this meant that vehicle weights crept up.

In the USA, the smooth six-cylinder engine was badly hit by tightening regulations, for peak power dropped from 90bhp in 1971 to a miserable 79bhp in 1973. Back at home, 104bhp in 1971 gave way to 98bhp in 1971 and to 95bhp in 1972. (The situation at Triumph's rival concern, MG, was equally as critical. The difference was that MG never admitted to the slide in power outputs...)

This private owner has customized his GT6 with appropriate mudflaps. Restoration of this corner of cars can be very time-consuming if mud and water have got into all the panel recesses around the tail-lamps.

In 1966 Triumph toyed with the idea of sending prototype racing GT6s to compete at Le Mans. Assembly of a test car got this far before the project was abandoned.

The GT6 Mk 3 was certainly the best of its type, and every road tester, in every country where the car was sold, seemed to have the same favourable opinions of the car. The fact is, however, that 5,062 cars were built in 1971, 4,695 in 1972 and only 2,745 in 1973.

British readers who have not studied the figures may wonder why the GT6 now seems to be so rare in the UK. In fact only 8,612 new GT6s were sold in the country between 1966 and 1973, which means an average of little more than 1,000 a year. The record sales year was 1967 (1,824 cars sold

– so much for the bleating of the press about the Mk 1...), with second and third best figures of 1,745 and 1,679 being achieved in the car's two final sales years, 1972 and 1973.

Before the car was finally pensioned-off, the 1973 model-year cars (those with Commission Numbers between KE (KF in the USA) 20001 and 34218) were given a final batch of improvements. The most surprising 'improvement' (for, at the time, some people did not see it as that) was the abandonment of the lower-wishbone rear suspension arrangement in favour of the cheaper and simpler swing-

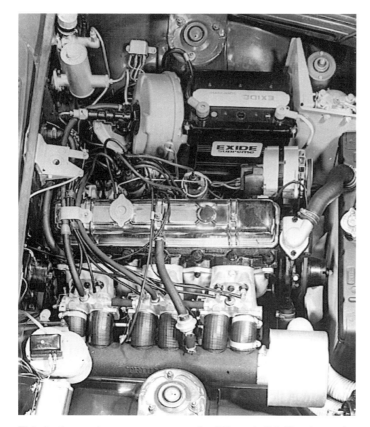

This is the engine compartment of a Triumph 2.5 PI saloon, the engine of which looks similar to that of a TR6. Several resourceful GT6 owners have managed to get the same engine into their cars, but its effect on the transmission can be imagined...

spring swing-axle layout of the Spitfire Mk IV.

Even though the swing-spring system was theoretically not as effective as the lower-wishbone system, practical tests showed that ride, roadholding and feel were all very similar, and I doubt if any non-technical customer would have noticed any difference. Indeed, I am quite sure that few such customers even knew there *had* been a change.

Production of the GT6 ran down rapidly in the summer of 1973, with only 193 cars built in the first half of October, 34 in the last week of that month, two more cars in mid-November and the final two just before the end of that month.

Why was the GT6 killed-off when the Spitfire soldiered on happily for another seven years? In fairness, I would say that it was not so much killed, as died of neglect. There were several reasons, the three most important being the onset of the Energy Crisis, the fast-growing mountain of USA safety legislation which would have to be satisfied in future years, and the fact that sales in the USA had been falling away since 1968.

There is evidence that British Leyland's planners were already preparing a comprehensive clear-out of old models so that the 'Bullet' project – it would be named Triumph TR7 when launched in 1975 – could have a clear run at the marketplace in the USA. It is also certain that the huge cost of keeping abreast with the USA legislation was no longer seen to be worth it – several other sports cars were being withdrawn from the United States at about the same time.

After seven years and more than 41,000 cars, therefore, the GT6's career was cut short. For years afterwards it was nearly forgotten, but in the 1980s it was soon seen as a 'different' sporting car, the result being that classic values rose sharply and many examples were restored and cosseted by their young owners.

CHAPTER 7

Blood relations – Herald and Vitesse

Canley-built breadwinners

As I have already explained in Chapter 1, the Spitfire and GT6 models were directly related to the Herald and Vitesse family. The Herald came before the Spitfire, the Vitesse came before the GT6, and in later years there was a co-ordinated development policy for all these types.

This short section lists where, when and how the various Heralds and Vitesses were produced:

Herald

The original Triumph Herald – coded 'Zobo' – was launched in April 1959, with a 948cc engine and a choice of two-door saloon or two-door coupe body styles.

This was the car which established Triumph's 1960s separate-chassis pedigree, and was the first to have the amazingly tight steering lock and offer the controversial swing-axle rear suspension.

For the first few weeks the coupe was in better supply than the saloon, but by mid-1959 the situation had reverted to normal. By comparison with the Spitfire (which would not be launched for another three years), the Heralds were heavier and less powerful. It is a miracle that several brave drivers managed to achieve success in rallies, notably Tiny Lewis and Geoff Mabbs in coupes.

At first the saloon had a single-carburettor 35bhp engine, while the coupe had a twin-carb 45bhp unit, but before long the twin-carb engine was also made available in the saloon as an optional extra.

Herald assembly (the cars were placed sideways, and closely packed, as they came down the final assembly line) was originally in the old Canley buildings (very close to the Canley railway station and level crossing), but Standard-Triumph's vast new assembly hall, 200 yards further west towards the Coventry bypass, took over that job before the end of 1960.

The Herald convertible, complete with twin-carburettor 45bhp engine, was launched in 1960, while the stripped-out, low-specification Herald S saloon went on sale in February 1961.

The first big shake-up, leading directly to the Spitfire, came in April 1961, when all except the Herald S became Herald 1200s – saloon, coupe and convertible, with a smart new three-door estate car version following a few weeks later. A light commercial vehicle version of the estate car, the Courier van, was launched in 1962. (The Herald S struggled on, theoretically, until 1964, but very few were sold...)

The Herald 1200 was a faster, more torquey and better-built car than the original, and certainly helped restore Standard-Triumph's flagging fortunes. All versions had the same single-carb 39bhp engine at first, and front-wheel disc brakes (the same as those fitted as standard equipment to the Spitfire) soon became optional. Once the Vitesse (see below) was announced, the Herald also inherited the strengthened chassis-frame of the new car.

Next to appear was the Herald 12/50 saloon, complete with sunroof as standard, and a single-carb 51bhp version of the 1,147cc engine, which was launched in March 1963. From the autumn of 1964, too, the other Heralds were treated to uprated engines, which produced 48bhp instead of

The Herald coupe was the first car in the entire family to go into production. It was longer than the Spitfire and had 2+2 seating, but was definitely a sporting Triumph at the time.

The Triumph Herald saloon was the best seller from which all other Herald/Vitesse/Spitfire/GT6 models drew components. This was an original 1959 model, with 948cc engine and painted bumpers; it would be replaced by the Herald 1200 model in 1961.

Like the Herald, the Vitesse was also available as a convertible. This was an original 1962 model. The number-plates are false for photographic purposes only – the *real* 3 VC was a works TR4 rally car.

the original 39bhp.

The 12/50s were built until August 1967, and 1200s until June 1970, but from the autumn of 1967 there was another derivative, the Herald 13/60. As its title implied, this had a larger and more powerful engine. It was, in fact, an altogether better car than before.

The 13/60s were instantly recognizable by their new front-end styling, which used the same basic pressings as the slant-headlamped Vitesse, but with only two large (7in diameter) headlamps. Saloon, convertible and estate types were available, and once they appeared the Herald 12/50 was dropped and the 1200 range reduced, only the 1200 saloon henceforth being built.

Under the skin, too, there were several worthwhile improvements, notably the use of a single-carb, 61bhp, 1,296cc engine, complete with the eight-port cylinder-head (closely related to that of the Spitfire Mk 3). Also as on the Spitfire, front wheel disc brakes were standardized.

By the end of the run, Heralds had been assembled, from CKD packs, in Australia, Belgium, India, New Zealand, Peru and Portugal. The last UK-produced Herald of all, a 13/60, was built at Canley in May 1971, though Indian Gazels were built until 1973.

Vitesse
Work began on six-cylinder-engined/separate-chassis cars in 1957 (this was 'Zebu', which might have succeeded the Vanguard), but these were altogether larger than the Heralds, and all were cancelled before they progressed beyond the prototype stage.

The Vitesse – project-coded 'Atom' – came into existence in 1960 when technical chief Harry Webster demanded a faster car than his habitual Herald coupe. The first prototype, therefore, had a 2-litre engine in a Herald coupe shell, and was always known as the 'Kenilworth dragster'. Harry lived in Kenilworth...Prototypes were built in 1961, and the original car, the Vitesse 1600, was launched in May 1962. Naturally, the Vitesse was closely based on the Herald layout, but in addition to the use of a six-cylinder engine there were many other important differences:

The Vitesse had a different front-end style, which featured a different bonnet shape and four headlamps set in a slant-eyed position. The chassis-frame, though visually similar to that of the Herald 1200, was much more rigid in many ways, particularly at the front end and where it supported the final-drive casing. This frame, suitably modified in the engine mountings area, was subsequently standardized in the Herald.

The engine was a 1.6-litre/70bhp version of the Vanguard Six unit, and because of its length it was mounted well

The Herald 13/60 facia used several components which should be familiar to Spitfire owners of the period, notably the steering wheel and some of the switchgear.

The Vitesse 2-litre model had an engine which was almost identical to that fitted to the GT6 of the day.

This was the Herald 13/60 estate car, complete with a single-carb version of the 1,296cc engine which was used in Spitfires for some years, along with the same gearbox, back axle and basic suspension components.

The Vitesse 2-litre Mk 2 had the same engine as the GT6 Mk 2, along with the same very effective swing-spring rear suspension installation.

forward in the chassis-frame. As with the GT6, it was a *very* close fit...

The gearbox, though visually the same as that of the Herald, had close ratios; Laycock overdrive was optional. The rear axle, too, was a more robust version of the Herald unit. Front disc brakes were standard.

The Vitesse 1600 was available in saloon or convertible form, but was never officially built as a coupe or an estate car. Later in its run, the 1600 was given a more completely equipped instrument panel (from September 1963), and a more powerful engine (Zenith-Stromberg carbs instead of semi-downdraught Solex, from mid-1965).

The Vitesse 2-litre took over from the 1600 in the autumn of 1966. As before, it was sold as a two-door saloon or a two-door convertible.

Compared with the 1600, the 2-litre had a 1,998cc/95bhp six-cylinder engine, to which a new all-synchromesh four-speed gearbox and a yet more robust rear axle were mated. This power train, of course, was shared with the GT6, which was introduced at the same time. Wider-rim wheels and larger front disc brakes were also standardized.

The 2-litre then gave way to the 2-litre Mk 2 from the autumn of 1968, sharing all its improvements with the GT6 Mk 2, which was launched on the same day. The Mk 2, in other words, had a more powerful engine and the effective

The Bond Equipe 1300 GT4S was built at Preston in the late 1960s with an intriguing mixture of Herald and Spitfire running gear, some Herald bodywork, but many unique glassfibre panels.

This is the Bond Equipe 2-litre, which used a Vitesse 2-litre chassis and some GT6 components under its glassfibre skin.

lower-wishbone type of independent rear suspension. Compared with the GT6, however, the Vitesse used lever-arm rear dampers, which were actually transversely mounted, fixed to the chassis-frame behind the line of the drive-shafts.

The last Mk 2 saloons were built in March 1971, the last of the convertibles following in May 1971.

Total production of Heralds and Vitesses between 1959 and 1971 was as follows:

948cc saloon	86,129
948cc coupe	15,157
948cc convertible	8,258
948cc saloon 'S'	6,577
1200 saloon	201,143
1200 coupe	5,312
1200 convertible	43,299
1200 estate	39,821
Courier van	5,136
12/50 saloon	54,807

13/60 saloon	49,443
13/60 convertible	16,091
13/60 estate	17,118
Vitesse 1600 saloon	22,818
Vitesse 1600 convertible	8,459
Vitesse 1600 coupe	1 **
Vitesse 2-litre saloon (Mk 1 and Mk 2)	12,978
Vitesse 2-litre Mk 2 convertible (Mk 1 and Mk 2)	6,974

**This model never officially existed...

The production total for Herald-type Standard Gazels built in India is not known.

Vitesse estate cars were never officially produced, and none were ever built at Canley. A few cars, however, were later created at the Standard-Triumph London Service Centre by combining the appropriate Vitesse chassis with Herald 1200 estate car rear-end shells.

CHAPTER 8

The practical side – chassis and mechanical

Strip-down, renovation and rebuilding

In many cases modern cars are more difficult to restore than older types, usually because their design and construction is much more complicated. Today's unit-construction cars may be more rigid, stronger and cheaper to build than traditional machines with separate chassis, but restorers hate working on them.

On the other hand, rebuilding a Spitfire or a GT6 is quite a straightforward business as the bodyshell can be split from the chassis and running gear, and because neither provides *all* the strength for the complete structure, you can separate them to carry out some work before having to bring them together again.

That, I am sure, is one of the reasons why Spitfire and GT6 restoration is such a thriving business as the classic car boom reaches maturity, and I am sure it explains why such a high proportion of the spare parts are now available for this work to be done.

There is a such a lot of readily available information and advice about restoration that I have decided to provide two complete sections – one about the mechanical side and one about the bodywork. Even so, this is not meant to be a detailed account of the restoration process – there is certainly no blow-by-blow analysis – but rather an overview of the problems you can overcome.

Strip-down

As I have already made clear in earlier chapters, the layout of any member of the Herald/Vitesse/Spitfire/GT6 family is simple, and it is possible to consider any of the cars as a vast construction or Meccano kit. Where other 1960s cars tended to be welded together, these Triumphs seemed to be bolted together instead.

When tackling a restoration, therefore, it is somewhat easier than on most other cars to split the car into its important sections, and to tackle restoration in more comfort. Just so long as you have spacious premises – or somewhere to store everything when it is taken off the car – you should soon be able to get good access to any feature of it.

At the start of a major rebuild it is always desirable to remove the body from the rolling chassis, and I recommend this. However, once work on the frame is complete you should then use it as a ready-made jig or pattern to bolt back to the body while that is being restored.

Why is this? You should remember that the backbone frame adds a lot of stiffness to the shell itself, which means that the shell is far more likely to distort if the frame is removed and the shell is not properly stored or supported.

In fact, various experts have told me that the bodyshell, once removed, should preferably be laid on a flat floor, or a similar working surface, and that any restoration work involving welding (and possible distortion) should be carried out with the frame in place.

Before starting to split the shell from the chassis, or removing major sections from the assembly, remember to disconnect electrical, hydraulic, or cable lines where appropriate. The car, after all, was designed to plug together, so it has also been designed to strip down in the same way.

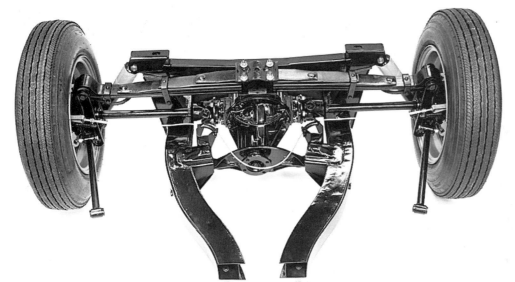

This was the later swing-spring type of rear suspension as used in Spitfire Mk IV and 1500 types, and for the 1973 model of the GT6. The effect was to give very little roll stiffness, but the usual resistance to single-wheel bump loads. It worked very well indeed. Restoration work is usually confined to renewing bushes and bearings.

There is a good supply of parts for restoring Spitfire engines, even though the car has been out of production since 1980. For routine maintenance work, it is often advisable to remove the splash-guards at each side of the engine so that access to the starter, generator and other details is much easier.

Water and muck often collects on the chassis-frame immediately ahead of the bulkhead pressings, which eventually rust through, as does the bulkhead supporting the wiper motor and the master cylinders.

It helps to remove the bonnet, then remove the front lower panel right away. Not only will this make it easier to get at the front end of the running gear, but it also means that these big panels can be removed and stored away from the rest of the car.

How and where does the bodyshell unbolt? There are 10 body bolts. To locate them, have a look at the workshop manual, which gives full details – the ones you might miss are at the back (above the differential) and the two under the seats. Remember, of course, that the rear suspension radius-arms also bolt up direct to the floorpan (behind the seats), and that the rear dampers on lower-wishbone rear suspension GT6s also have a bodyshell (rather than a chassis) fixing.

Except that you must remove the steering column assembly first, the bodyshell can be removed without disturbing any other major aspect of the rolling chassis.

Once the shell has been removed, a detailed strip-down can be completed in the normal way. Now it is time to get started on the restoration.

Chassis-frame

First of all, reassure yourself that the frame is still square (there are workshop manual diagrams and dimensions to give guidance here), that it has not been in an accident, and has not been bodge-repaired. On these frames it is very easy to nudge a front corner out of line, although the rear end of the frame should be safe. If you noticed that the bonnet/scuttle fitting line was askew, or different from one side to the other, this *may* already have given you a clue.

On old cars there will be a lot of old gunge, paint or underseal splattered indiscriminately around the frame. If you are serious about a restoration it is always advisable to

101

take the frame back to bare metal. You may uncover horrors, but be glad that this was the stage at which they became obvious.

Bad rust tends to occur at the front outriggers which hold the bonnet pivot points. Front suspension towers (these are bolt-on items) may have been bent in accidents, but generally they do not rust badly. Front body outriggers (under the footwells) sometimes rust where they join the main backbone members, but the smaller outriggers rarely give trouble. This is the time to consider adding strengthening patches to the outriggers and bonnet pivot points.

Main backbone members are usually sound, but of course these can be plated where necessary. Rusting sometimes occurs under the line of the rear drive-shafts, where water may have been standing for some time during the car's earlier life.

After repair and renovation, experts recommend having the rebuilt frame pressure grit-blasted, then zinc-coated (to ensure long life), followed by powder coating and Waxoyl treatment.

Suspension and steering
Old Spitfires tend to creak, rattle and squeak, and many of those noises are concentrated in the suspension and steering areas. Except for stopping the corrosion of the bodies, the rectification of these areas is probably the most worthwhile of all.

The front suspension/steering assembly suffers from a series of worn joints, bushes and bearings. If you are serious about a proper rebuild, budget for replacing all of them. If I must pick the worst culprit in this area, it is the trunnion in the vertical link (old-fashioned readers would call this the kingpin...); the reason for rapid wear is that this is one of the few parts of the Spitfire which needs regular lubrication, but is often forgotten, or neglected by owners of the older cars.

The steering should be light and accurate. On worn-out cars steering precision suffers from worn ball-joints at each end of the track-rods, or from floppy rubber mountings between the rack and the chassis. The rack itself is usually in much better condition than the rest of the steering assembly.

The rear suspension can also suffer from a multitude of worn joints and bushes. On simple swing-axle cars the handling can be spooky enough, even when everything is bolted down correctly; when there is wear, or sloppiness in the joints, the results can be a bit perturbing.

The noise usually comes from worn bushes in the outer vertical links, and at each end of the radius-arms, though damper bushes also wear out and add to the general imprecision.

During a rebuild, if you are tempted to fit new road springs, either at the front or the rear, be sure to consult an expert and get precisely the correct spring for the model. Any of the springs fitted to any of the separate-chassis Triumph cars *could* fit, but there are several different rates and (in the case of the transverse leaf springs) different cambers.

Generally speaking, these cars handle best of all when their rear springs provide a touch of negative camber in normal motoring conditions; some leaf springs provide this as fitted, others do not. If your car sits up quite high at the rear, I genuinely think it is worth the effort of fitting a different spring, or having the existing one decambered.

On lower-wishbone GT6s, the Rotoflex couplings fitted to the rear drive-shafts have a hard job to do – they have to deal with torque *and* shaft 'plunge' – so an owner should always be prepared to renew these. They tend to crack up around the bolt holes, and in certain circumstances the bonding between the rubber and the metal sleeves begins to break down.

Many of these cars are fitted with centre-lock wire-spoke wheels. After a lot of hard use these wheels tend to develop loose spokes, and their drive spines (particularly at the rear) tend to wear badly. Fortunately, replacement wire wheels are still made, and dodgy wheels can be refurbished.

Engines and transmissions
Except in the area of the rear axle, where special advice applies, there is nothing unconventional, or unexpected, about the engines and transmissions fitted to these cars.

Because the Spitfire engines were fitted to late-model MG Midgets, and because MG fanatics objected to this, there has been a serious 'whispering campaign' against the Spitfire engines in recent years. This is wrong – in fact I would suggest that it is maliciously wrong.

Spitfires and GT6s which have been in accidents often suffer from creased chassis members. When buying a car, have a careful look at exposed members, like those below and ahead of the radiator.

The Triumph Sports Six Club is growing all the time, and all Spitfire and GT6 owners should join it. Its advice on restoration and parts supply is invaluable.

The Triumph SC engines (like the BMC A-Series engines fitted to earlier Midgets) are as reliable as the service and care they get. Any engine, after all, which was basically good enough to win its capacity class in 24-hour races, and to outlast the Alpine-Renaults in the Tour de France, is basically sound.

On all the engines – four-cylinder and six-cylinder – your original investigations should concentrate on the oil pressure, the general sound of the valve gear and the condition of the exhaust. I take it for granted that you will have the twin carburettors (a single-carb on some North American-tune cars) set up and even rebuilt if necessary.

A hot engine which doesn't generate the recommended oil pressure (appropriate figures, in each case, are in the factory literature) probably has worn crankshaft bearings, allied to an oil pump which has seen better days. Noisy valve gear – rockers, tappets, or stretched camshaft drive chains all contribute – means reduced performance and economy. In

Any Spitfire and GT6 owner should try to purchase suitable workshop manuals and parts lists to support his or her hobby.

old age all these engines use more oil around worn valve guides, pistons and cylinder walls; a smokey exhaust tells its own story.

On Mk 1, 2 and 3 Spitfires, the gearboxes have quite a hard time. In old age they will certainly have lost much of their synchromesh, some of the precision of their selector linkage, and there will often be a distressing tendency to jump out of reverse gear. There is no easy fix for any of these problems, but complete rebuilds, and all spare parts, are available.

The late-model Spitfires and the GT6s have the more robust all-synchromesh gearbox, which does a better job and stands up better to old age and a lot of use. There is no tendency to jump out of gears on this design. When new, the change quality was often described as 'notchy', but worn selector bushes and forks allowed most gearboxes to become quite sloppy as they grew old.

Many Spitfires and GT6s have Laycock overdrive, and from time to time these seem to stop working. Most overdrive malfunctions are caused by failures to the external electrical solenoid (water and other road filth has a lot to answer for...), or by the clogging-up of internal hydraulic control passages. The DIY owner can deal with a solenoid failure by fitting another, but a clogged-up unit must be completely rebuilt by an expert.

There are so many different combinations of back axle,

The solenoid on this Laycock overdrive needs replacing. That's a common problem on old Spitfires and GT6s, but the change is straightforward enough.

propeller shaft, output shaft and output flange on this family of cars that I have published a chart in Appendix D. From this chart you will see that some Spitfire back-ends are more robust than others – the earlier Spitfires being weaker than later cars – but that all 1970s cars are as strong as reasonably possible.

Unless an owner is looking for an absolutely authentic rebuild, I see no reason why late-model parts should not be used in earlier cars; with a bit of forethought, this is always possible and, I suggest, not to be condemned.

Rebuilding

If you plan carefully ahead, it should be possible to phase a restoration so that the chassis-frame can be used to stiffen-up the bodyshell while this is being restored, before once again being removed for the complete drive-line and suspensions to be re-installed.

CHAPTER 9

The practical side – bodywork

Chasing the rust bug

I am afraid to say that most Spitfires and GT6s need a lot of regular attention to make sure their bodies don't rust away persistently and disastrously. Cars which have already had one proper restoration in recent years (using modern anti-corrosion treatment to make sure the dreaded tin-worm doesn't strike again too readily) seem to last a lot longer than the originals ever did.

There's nothing to be ashamed of here, for the sporting Triumphs were really no worse – nor any better – built than any other British car of the period. The bodywork of these cars, at least, is quite straightforward to restore; you'll notice I did not say easy.

Strip-down
As I have already written in the previous chapter, to restore all the mechanical aspects of the Spitfire/GT6 cars, it is best to remove the bodyshell, the front valance and the entire lift-up bonnet section from the chassis before beginning. However, I also explained that the backbone chassis contributes a lot to the overall stiffness of the shell, so after the chassis has been removed it is advisable to store the shell (particularly of an open-top Spitfire) on a flat surface to ensure that it is not encouraged to distort or sag in the middle.

Complete new bodyshells are no longer available to help a no-expense-spared rebuild, but almost every individual panel, or sub-section, *is* on the market, from one source or another, to help an owner complete his repairs. One of Britain's biggest parts suppliers – Moss Europe, which has six branches – recently showed me a Spitfire Mk IV/1500 parts list in which almost every body panel or sub-section was illustrated, listed and priced.

Because the Mk IV/1500 type of shell had a completely different skin from that of the original type, it is more difficult to find new panels for these earlier and therefore very much older cars, but with patience it *can* be done.

What to look for
No two cars are alike, nor corrode exactly the same way, but almost all exhibit the same general habits. At restoration time, therefore, I think my general advice is accurate:

First of all, let's consider the original type of shell, as fitted to Spitfires Mks 1, 2 and 3 and (in fastback form) to GT6 Mks 1 and 2.

The bonnet assembly is particularly vulnerable to corrosion, not only because it is a big and rather unwieldy structure which seems to invite distortion, but because of its construction. Danger spots are the panel edges around the headlamp mountings, the side/indicator cutouts, and the cutouts around the bonnet latch points. The exposed seams are particularly vulnerable, as are the inner wheelarch joints and the edges of the outer wheelarches.

The front panel suffers a lot from stone chips, but there are no other bad corrosion spots.

On the main bodyshell, the inner/outer sills, the floor panels and the pick-up points for the rear suspension radius-arms are all likely to rot away, while the boot floor, the scuttle area around the base of the screen and the inner wheelarches

The closing panel at the corner of the Spitfire or GT6 bonnet often corrodes badly.

at the rear all give problems in old age. Most of these cars suffer badly from salt and filth thrown up by the rear wheels – both ahead of and behind the wheelarches.

You should also look for evidence of hydraulic spillage on the bulkhead in the region of the brake and clutch reservoirs, and for battery acid corrosion on the opposite side of the car.

Generally speaking, rust will always appear at exposed joints, particularly where these have been covered with brightwork, such as on the crown line of the rear wings, and it can be particularly bad in the base of the doors.

Special to the original-shape GT6 is the likelihood of corrosion on the roof panel (close to the joint with the windscreen surround), on the sides of the roof above the doors, and on the transverse panel seam across the tail. Leaky tailgates sometimes allow rust to start at the edges of the hatchback.

The reskinned body (Spitfires Mk IV/1500 and GT6 Mk 3) had a smoother and better-detailed bonnet assembly, but on the other hand there are bigger problems at the tail and on the front valance.

The bonnet itself suffers less from external corrosion, and less because it has fewer front-end cutouts, but there can still be serious problems around inner wheelarch joints and along the joint between the bonnet top and side panels. The front valance houses the side/indicator lamps, and for that reason seems to go rusty around the apertures.

The longer tail, with its cut-off style, brings problems of its own, especially around the stop/tail/indicator lamps and at the panel joints between inner and outer wheelarches and the tail panel itself.

On all these cars, it is best to assume that there will have been water leakage into the cabin at one time or another, either because an open-top Spitfire has been caught in the rain several times too often, or there has been water ingress around the door glasses, chassis fixing points, or the edges of the gearbox tunnel where the sealing has deteriorated. Sadly, this means that on older cars many items of trim, or the carpets, will have been soaked. These will all have to be replaced, and although original spare parts are long gone, high-quality pattern parts are now available.

Not quite as rare as hen's teeth, but definitely expensive! This is a line of GT6 bonnet assemblies – the Spitfire is the same except for the bonnet bulge and the louvres.

Re-assembly

Before offering up the bodyshell to the chassis, be sure that there is no likelihood of trapping any hydraulic or electrical lines between frame members and the body panels – use tape or tie-wraps to keep them away from trouble if this looks likely.

Be sure, too, that the bolt-down points on the chassis are clear of debris or (more likely in this case) fresh paint or underbody protection, and be sure that you have all the washers and spare packing pieces which you may need.

Fix the main bodyshell to the chassis before you even consider assembling the front-end, offer-up the bonnet next, and fit the front valance last of all. Unless you are very lucky, the initial bonnet/scuttle fit will leave something to be desired, and you will have to use every possible adjustment, or even make changes to the position of the front pivots; this sounds simple enough, but as it might involve three-dimensional adjustment it is best left to an expert!

This GT6 needed a lot of work around the doors, sills and rear quarter, but it will all be worth it in the end...

This Brazilian-owned Spitfire bodyshell is well on its way to restoration. This is the point at which a first-time restorer's heart begins to recover, if not his bank account!

A part-restored Spitfire 1500 which had needed new sills, front lower panel, bonnet side panel and much more... All such panels or sections are available.

On this car a patch panel had been needed behind the line of the rear wheel, along with the new rear cross panel. The chassis itself was still sound.

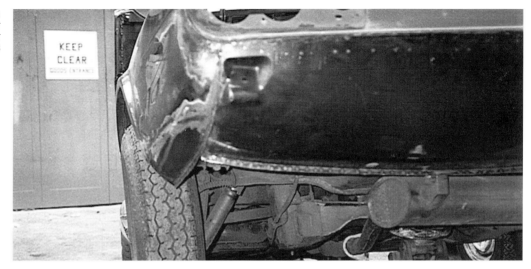

Old meets new. Much repair work had restored the strength of the sills when this shot was taken, the car being almost ready for repainting.

A sight to gladden the eyes of a restorer. This is a Spitfire whose bodyshell restoration had been completed, ready for painting to begin. Note the complex nature of the floorpan and the door inner panels.

On the Spitfire and GT6 the bonnet closes on to a 'skid panel' at the side of the footwell. This may wear and rust badly over the years.

Not a pretty sight. A Spitfire 1500 which has needed repairs to the pillar behind the door and will now need a complete new outer wing.

Scruffy, but restorable. This boot area at least appears to have been dry throughout its life.

CHAPTER 10

The club scene

From UK to USA and Australia

In the UK it is probably true to say that the Spitfire and GT6 models would never have reached their current classic status without the enthusiastic influence of the Triumph Sports Six Club.

This organization was set up in 1977 to cater for the owners of *all* the separate-chassis Herald/Vitesse/Spitfire/GT6 family of cars. Even though the Spitfire was still in production at that time, it had virtually been orphaned by British Leyland, and many of the older cars were rapidly rotting away as spares became more and more scarce. Officers of the fledgling club wanted to reverse that process.

After a slow start, the club expanded rapidly in the 1980s, such that a fully staffed office and administrators were needed. Every time I visited Bill Sunderland (the club manager) and Trudi Squibbs (office manager) in that decade, I found more and more records and activity, which was a measure of the way new members were appearing.

The TSSC soon outgrew its rented premises in the middle of Market Harborough, and eventually cast around for a permanent HQ. Early in 1991 the dream came true when the club was rehoused to this address:

Triumph Sports Six Club Ltd
Main Street
Lubenham
Market Harborough
Leicestershire LE16 9TF

Tel: 0858-434424   Fax: 0858-431936

I am confident that this important contact address will not change during the life of this book.

The TSSC is now the largest Triumph one-make club in the UK, and has links with other Triumph clubs all round the world. I have listed some of these below.

Activities? Apart from providing a very professional-looking monthly magazine (*The Courier*) and a regular special-interest survey of one particular model (*Turning Circle*), the club runs Registers for each of the derivatives (there are separate Registers for the Spitfire 1/2/3, Spitfire IV/1500, and GT6 ranges), and markets a whole series of literature (workshop manuals and parts lists in particular) to make maintenance and restoration easier.

It also offers valuation services on all the cars, operates a special car insurance service for members, provides advice on parts and service expertise, and has a very active social scene. Members also get involved in racing events, there is a video library, and a number of special offers are available.

It is no insult to *The Courier* to comment that its most fascinating section is the page after page of advertising from specialists who offer all manner of parts and services to maintain and rebuild the cars. These, and the separate advertising supplement published inside *The Courier*, mean that a TSSC member has no excuse for not being able to find parts or expertise to keep his car on the road.

Overseas links
When you think how many of these cars were originally sold in the USA, it is surprising that there is no Spitfire/GT6 one-

115

Can you pick all the models at this TSSC gathering? They include not only Spitfires and GT6s, but Triumph-chassis specials, TR7s, Stags, Dolomites, Vitesses and Heralds.

make club over there. Instead, enthusiasts are referred to the Spitfire/GT6 consultant of the Vintage Triumph Register, who is:

David Pelham
VTR
1900 Fairway Drive
Springfield
Illinois 62704
USA

Tel: (217) 546-2273

He, in turn, will probably put the owner in touch with one of no fewer than 35 different regional clubs in states as far-flung as California, Florida and Oregon.

The TSSC also lists two associate clubs in Australia, which are:

Triumph Sports Owners
  Association
Post Office Box 192
Glenside
South Australia 5065

Triumph Sports Owners
  Association
Post Office Box 147
Nedlands
Western Australia 6009

APPENDIX A

Technical specifications

Triumph Spitfires and GT6s had slightly different specifications for sale in different markets. In particular, in the 1970s the USA-market specification differed widely from that of UK-market cars.

Accordingly, the main tabular material quoted below is for home-market (UK) cars and – where applicable – the USA-market differences are quoted separately.

Spitfire Mk 1 – produced 1962 to 1964

Style: Two-door open-top sports car with optional hardtop. Separate backbone chassis and steel bodywork. Front engine and rear-wheel drive.

Engine: 4-cyl, ohv, 69.3 x 76mm, 1,147cc (2.73 x 2.99in, 70cu in), CR 9.0:1, 2 SU carbs. 63bhp (net) at 5,750rpm. Maximum torque 67lb/ft at 3,500rpm.

Transmission: Rear-wheel drive, 6.25in single-dry-plate clutch and four-speed gearbox (no synchromesh on first gear); from late 1963, optional overdrive on top and third gears. Axle ratio 4.11:1. Overall gear ratios 4.11 (3.37 on optional overdrive top), 5.74 (4.71 on optional overdrive third), 8.88, 15.42, reverse 15.42:1. 15.7mph/1,000rpm in top gear (19.1mph/1,000rpm in overdrive top gear).

Suspension, steering and brakes: Ifs, coil springs, wishbones, anti-roll bar and telescopic dampers. Irs, transverse leaf spring, swing-axles, radius-arms, telescopic dampers. Rack-and-pinion steering, 3.8 turns lock-to-lock. 9in front disc brakes, 7 x 1.25in rear drum brakes. 5.20–13in cross-ply tyres on 3.5in-rimmed steel disc wheels; optional 4.5in-rimmed centre-lock wire wheels from late 1963.

Dimensions: Wheelbase 6ft 11in (211cm); front track 4ft 1in (124.5cm); rear track 4ft 0in (122cm). Overall length 12ft 1in (368cm); width 4ft 9in (145cm); height 3ft 11.5in (120.5cm). Unladen weight (basic specification) 1,568lb (711kg).

UK retail price when new: £730, £641 from November 1962 when UK purchase tax levels reduced.

Spitfire Mk 2 – produced 1964 to 1967

Specification as for Mk 1, except for:

Engine: 67bhp (net) at 6,000rpm. Maximum torque 67lb/ft at 3,750rpm.

Transmission: 6.5in diaphragm-spring clutch.

UK retail price when new: £666.

Spitfire Mk 3 – produced 1967 to 1970

Specification as for Mk 2, except for:

Engine: 73.7 x 76mm, 1,296cc (2.90 x 2.99in, 79.1cu in). 75bhp (net) at 6,000rpm. Maximum torque 75lb/ft at 4,000rpm.

Suspension, steering and brakes: 4.5in-rimmed steel disc wheels for 1970 model year.

UK retail price when new: £717.

Spitfire Mk IV – produced 1970 to 1974

Specification as for Mk 3, except for:

Engine: 63bhp (DIN) at 6,000rpm. Maximum torque 69lb/ft at 3,500rpm.

Transmission: Four-speed all-synchromesh gearbox. Axle ratio 3.89:1. Overall gear ratios 3.89 (3.12 on optional overdrive top), 5.41 (4.34 on optional overdrive third), 8.41, 13.65, reverse 15.0:1. 16.7mph/1,000rpm in top gear (20.8mph/1,000rpm in overdrive top gear).
Suspension, steering and brakes: Irs, 'swing-spring'. Steering 3.5 turns lock-to-lock. 145–13in radial-ply tyres.
Dimensions: Rear track (for 1973 model year) 4ft 2in (127cm). Overall length 12ft 5in (378.5cm); width 4ft 10.5in (148.5cm). Unladen weight (basic specification) 1,717lb (779kg).
UK retail price when new: £962.

Spitfire 1500 – produced 1974 to 1980

Specification as for Mk IV, except for:
Engine: 73.7 x 87.5mm, 1,493cc (2.90 x 3.44in, 91.1cu in). 71bhp (DIN) at 5,500rpm. Maximum torque 82lb/ft at 3,000rpm.
Transmission: Axle ratio 3.63:1. Overall gear ratios 3.63 (2.90 on optional overdrive top), 5.05 (4.03 on optional overdrive third), 7.84, 12.70, reverse 13.99:1. 18.0mph/1,000rpm in top gear (22.6mph/1,000rpm in overdrive top gear).
Suspension, steering and brakes: 155–13in tyres. 5in rims from late 1978.
Dimensions: Unladen weight (basic specification) 1,750lb (794kg).
UK retail price when new: £1,360.
UK retail price when discontinued in 1980: £4,524.

Specification differences for USA-market cars
Until 1968 the UK/European and USA specifications were virtually the same, then:

1969
Engine: CR 8.5:1, 68bhp (net) at 5,500rpm. Maximum torque 73lb/ft at 3,000rpm.
Dimensions: Unladen weight 1,652lb (749kg).

1970
Engine: As 1969, but CR 9:1. One Zenith-Stromberg carb.

1971 as 1970, except for:
Engine: 58bhp (net) at 5,200rpm. Maximum torque 72lb/ft at 3,000rpm.

1972 as 1971, except for:
Engine: CR 8:1. 48bhp (net) at 5,500rpm. Maximum torque 61lb/ft at 2,900rpm.
Transmission: Rear axle ratio 4.11:1, intermediate ratios accordingly lower.

1973 as 1972, except for:
Engine: 1,493cc (as later Spitfire 1500), CR 7.5:1. 57bhp (net) at 5,000rpm. Maximum torque 74lb/ft at 3,000rpm.
Transmission: Axle ratio to reverted to 3.89:1 (as UK-spec cars).

1974 as 1973, but with wider, 155–13in tyres.

1975 as 1974 specification, but unladen weight 1,828lb (829kg).

1976 as 1975, but engine CR 9:1.

1977 as 1976, but engine CR 7.5:1 and exhaust catalyst fitted.

1978 as 1977, but unladen weight 1,850lb (839kg).

1979 as 1978, but because of use of energy absorbing bumpers, overall length 13ft 1.5in (400cm).

1980 as 1979, but weight 1,875lb (850kg). Car no longer sold in California, where emission regulations were even tighter than for other US states.

GT6 Mk 1 – produced 1966 to 1968
Style: Two-door sports coupe/hatchback. Separate backbone chassis and steel bodywork. Front engine and rear-wheel drive.
Engine: 6-cyl, ohv, 74.7 x 76mm, 1,998cc (2.94 x 2.99in, 122cu in), CR 9.5:1, 2 Zenith-Stromberg carbs. 95bhp (net) at 5,000rpm. Maximum torque 117lb/ft at 3,000rpm.

Transmission: Rear-wheel drive, 8.5in diaphragm-spring clutch and four-speed all-synchromesh gearbox; optional overdrive on top and third gears. Axle ratio 3.27:1, 3.89:1 with overdrive fitted. Overall gear ratios without overdrive 3.27, 4.11, 5.82, 8.66, reverse 10.13:1. With overdrive, 3.11 (O/d top), 3.89, 4.86 (O/d third), 6.92, 10.30, reverse 12.06:1. 20.1mph/1,000rpm in (non-overdrive) top gear, 21.2mph/1,000rpm in overdrive top gear.

Suspension, steering and brakes: Ifs, coil springs, wishbones, anti-roll bar and telescopic dampers. Irs, transverse leaf spring, swing-axles, radius-arms, telescopic dampers. Rack-and-pinion steering, 4.25 turns lock-to-lock. 9.7in front disc brakes, 8 x 1.25in rear drum brakes. 155–13in radial-ply tyres on 4.5in-rimmed steel disc wheels; optional 4.5in-rimmed centre-lock wire wheels.

Dimensions: Wheelbase 6ft 11in (211cm); front track 4ft 1in (124.5cm); rear track 4ft 0in (122cm). Overall length 12ft 1in (368cm); width 4ft 9in (145cm); height 3ft 11in (119.5cm). Unladen weight (basic specification) 1,904lb (865kg).

UK retail price when new: £985.

GT6 Mk 2 – produced 1968 to 1970

Specification as for GT6 Mk 1, except for:
Engine: CR 9.25:1. 104bhp (net) at 5,000rpm. Maximum torque 117lb/ft at 3,000rpm.
Transmission: Early cars had 3.27:1 rear axle ratio with or without overdrive. Overall gear ratios with overdrive 2.62 (O/d top), 3.27, 3.29 (O/d third), 4.11, 5.82, 8.66, reverse 10.13:1. 25.2mph/1,000rpm in overdrive top gear.
Suspension, steering and brakes: Irs, transverse leaf spring, reverse lower wishbones, radius-arms, telescopic dampers. Dimensions: Rear track 4ft 1in (124.5cm).
UK retail price when new: £1,148.

GT6 Mk 3 – produced 1970 to 1973

Specification as for GT6 Mk 2, except for:
Transmission: All cars with 3.27:1 rear axle (non-overdrive) or 3.89:1 (with optional overdrive).
Suspension, steering and brakes: For 1973 model year (launched February 1973), irs by transverse leaf 'swing-spring', swing-axles, radius-arms, telescopic dampers.
Dimensions: Overall length 12ft 5in (378.5cm); rear track for 1973 4ft 2in (127cm). Width 4ft 10.5in (148.5cm). Unladen weight (basic specification) 2,030lb (921kg).

Specification differences for USA-market cars:

There were no significant differences before 1969, then:

1969 and 1970 – car called 'GT6 Plus'.
Engine: 95bhp (net) at 4,700rpm. Maximum torque 117lb/ft at 3,400rpm.
Transmission: Where overdrive was specified, it was always matched to a 3.89:1 rear axle.

1971 as 1970 except for:
Engine: 90bhp (net) at 4,700rpm. Maximum torque 116lb/ft at 3,400rpm.

1972 and 1973 as 1971 except for:
Engine: CR 8:1. 79bhp (net) at 4,900rpm. Maximum torque 97lb/ft at 2,900rpm.

APPENDIX B

Production figures

Exactly how many Spitfires and GT6s were built? Who knows? I'm not certain, the British Motor Industry Heritage Trust isn't sure, and the Rover/BL/British Leyland organization has stated different things at different times!

The more I write about cars, the less I am sure about the production figures I am obliged to quote. These days, with computers and other sophisticated recording methods, you would think it is easy – but not in this case.

To see how difficult it is to be precise about Spitfire and GT6 figures, consider the following:

Claimed annual production figures

Total production	Figures provided in 1982	Figures provided by BL in 1985
Spitfire	314,152	314,342
GT6	40,926	41,253

Production by model

Spitfire Mk 1	45,573	45,754
Spitfire Mk 2	37,409	37,408
Spitfire Mk 3	65,320	
Spitfire Mk IV	70,021	}140,043*
Spitfire 1500	95,829	91,137
GT6 Mk 1	15,818	Marks
GT6 Mk 2	12,066	not
GT6 Mk 3	13,042	separated – total 41,253**

* The split between Mk 3 and Mk IV was not provided.
** No split between Marks was provided.

The following, however, is the year-on-year breakdown and seems to be both detailed and consistent:

Annual production figures (calendar year)

Year	Home	Export	CKD	Total
Spitfire Mk 1				
1962	475	856	24	1,355
1963	3,685	14,661	2,604	20,950
1964	4,965	16,022	2,400	23,387
1965	0	38	24	62
Total	9,125	31,577	5,052	45,754
Spitfire Mk 2				
1965	4,348	12,220	3,336	19,904
1966	4,416	9,949	2,712	17,077
1967	238	189	0	427
Total	9,002	22,358	6,048	37,408
Spitfire Mk 3 and Mk IV (and first 1500s)				
1967	5,182	5,881	3,745	14,808
1968	4,563	15,036	***	19,599
1969	3,704	10,118	4,752	18,574
1970	4,534	12,507	***	17,041
1971	5,328	11,349	3,900	20,577
1972	7,077	12,679	***	19,756
1973	4,082	11,607	***	15,689
1974	2,743 ****	11,256 ****	***	13,999
Total	37,213	90,433	(12,397)	140,043

*** CKD production believed to be included in general export figure in these years. See also GT6 below.
**** Figures believed to include first non-USA 1500 models.

Spitfire 1500 (except for 1974 start-up):

Year				
1975	2,627	12,964	–	15,591
1976	4,117	14,792	–	18,909
1977	3,117	14,599	–	17,716
1978	4,145	17,044	–	21,189
1979	935	9,341	–	10,276
1980	1,164	6,292	–	7,456
Total	16,105	75,032	–	91,137

GT6

Year				
1966	68	934	432	1,434
1967	1,824	4,828	714	7,366
1968	771	6,247	***	7,018
1969	713	5,749	528	6,990
1970	622	4,781	***	5,403
1971	1,190	4,100	312	5,602
1972	1,745	2,950	***	4,695
1973	1,679	1,066	***	2,745
Total	8,612	30,655	(1,986)	41,253

CKD stands for 'Completely Knocked Down' and refers to cars exported in kit form for final assembly in an overseas factory. Triumph's CKD operation appears to have been closed down by 1974.

For the statistician (or the zealot?) there are several niggling inconsistencies between these figures, and the Commission Number sequences quoted in Appendix C: Car identification. In addition, the start-up and close-down points of various Spitfire Marks differ slightly from those provided in earlier years.

Pity the poor historian...

APPENDIX C

Car identification

Whereas most car manufacturers refer to Chassis Numbers, Standard-Triumph always identified a Spitfire or a GT6 by its Commission Number. Each model was identified as follows:

Model	Commission Number sequence
Spitfire Mk 1	FC1 to FC44656
Spitfire Mk 2	FC50001 to FC88904
Spitfire Mk 3	FD1 to FD15306. Then FD20000 to FD51967. Then (from October 1969) FD75000 to FD92803
Spitfire Mk IV	FH3 to FH64995 (FK prefix used for USA 1300s, FL prefix for Sweden and FM prefix for USA 1500s)
Spitfire 1500	FH75001 onwards FM28001U onwards (USA markets) FM28001UC onwards (California market only)
GT6 Mk 1	KC1 to KC13752
GT6 Mk 2	KC50001 to KC58046. Then (from October 1969) KC75001 to KC83397
GT6 Mk 3	KE00001 to KE04596 (1971 models) KE10001 to KE14816 (1972 models) KE20001 to KE24218 (1973 models) (USA-market cars carried a KF prefix)

This information was provided by Anders Clausager at

BMIHT in 1990 and double-checked with him. However, Anders and I agree that this raises as many questions as it answers. Here are some examples:

More Spitfire Mk 1s seem to have been built than Commission Numbers issued – 45,754 cars made, 44,656 numbers issued.

Conversely, *fewer* Mk 2s seem to have been made than Commission Numbers issued – 37,408 cars made, 38,904 numbers issued.

In the case of GT6s, not all Commission Numbers seem to have been taken up and allocated to cars – if they had been, a total of 43,825 GT6s would have been made, which compares with the probable production total of 41,235!

Chassis-frames

The backbone chassis-frame used as the foundation of Spitfire and GT6 models was unique to those cars; differences between the two cars were confined to mountings and braces to support different engine and radiator positions.

Heralds and Vitesses had entirely different frames. The only shared components were the bolt-on front suspension towers and the support brackets for the rear axle casings.

Front suspension and front brakes

Once the Spitfire and GT6 family was established, the whole separate-chassis Triumph family of cars shared the same basic front suspension layout and components.

There were several different braking installations (different discs and different calipers), and in general Spitfires and Heralds share the same components, while GT6s and Vitesse 2-litre models share an uprated installation.

Note: There are so many small differences between different types of Spitfire and GT6 that it would be folly to delve deeper in this Appendix. In all cases, restorers should arm themselves with the appropriate parts lists before beginning a rebuild.

APPENDIX D

Related models and component interchangeability

As I have already explained, the Spitfire and GT6 were closely related to the Herald/Vitesse family of cars. This Appendix deals with engines, transmissions and suspension components, noting their origin and use in other cars.

Engines

Four-cylinder

The origin of the Spitfire's four-cylinder engine dates from the early 1950s, when an all-new small Standard – the Eight – was designed. This car was always coded as the SC (Small Car). Its engine was an overhead-valve design, with three crankshaft main bearings.

The first version was an 803cc unit, but over the years it was gradually expanded to 1,493cc by changes to the cylinder bore, stroke and the cylinder-centre positions in the block. Engines of this type were in mass production from 1953 to 1980.

These were the principal types:

Capacity	Bore x stroke	Applications
803cc	58 x 76mm	Standard Eight from 1953
948cc	63 x 76mm	Standard Ten, Pennant and Triumph Herald from 1954
1,147cc	69.3 x 76mm	Herald 1200, 12/50 and Triumph Spitfire from 1961
1,296cc	73.7 x 76mm	Herald 13/60, Spitfire, Triumph 1300, Toledo, Dolomite 1300 from 1965

Many parts of this engine and gearbox, from a Herald 1200, are common with Spitfire items.

The Vitesse 1600 unit has a number of items in common with the original GT6, but the cylinder block and head details are different.

This is the rear-drive Triumph 1500TC saloon engine installation, where many major items and any number of small components are interchangeable with Spitfire 1500 components.

1,493cc	73.7 x 87.5mm	Triumph 1500, Spitfire, Dolomite 1500 and MG Midget 1500 from 1970

Along the way its peak power output increased from 28bhp (net) – about 24bhp (DIN) – in the Standard Eight to 71bhp (DIN) in the Spitfire 1500. Highly-tuned versions of the 1,296cc unit produced nearly 120bhp in rallying trim.

These engines were also sold to small independent manufacturers, notably Fairthorpe, TVR and Amphicar.

Six-cylinder

The six-cylinder engine used in the GT6 was a developed version of that first seen in the Standard Vanguard Six of 1960. This, in turn, was a six-cylinder version of the SC four-cylinder engine, using some common components, many castings and forgings being machined on the same transfer line machinery.

Like the 'four', the 'six' was a conventional cast-iron overhead-valve engine and had four crankshaft main bearings.

The first version was a 1,998cc engine, but larger and smaller versions were produced in the years which followed. The first such engine was used in 1960, the last (in the larger Triumph saloons) in 1977. These were the principal types:

Capacity	Bore x stroke	Applications
1,596cc	66.75 x 76mm	Triumph Vitesse 1600 from 1962 to 1966
1,998cc	74.7 x 76mm	Standard Vanguard Six, Triumph 2000, Vitesse 2-litre and GT6 from 1960
2,498cc	74.7 x 95mm	Triumph TR5, TR6, 2.5PI, 2500TC and 2500S from 1967

The Vitesse 1600 engine produced 70bhp (gross) – about 60bhp (net), the Vanguard Six's 2-litre engine produced 80bhp (net), and the most powerful version of all, as fitted to the original TR6 sports car, produced 150bhp (net).

Such six-cylinder engines were also supplied to Fairthorpe TVR and other small independent concerns.

Gearboxes

Three different four-speed types were fitted to Spitfire and GT models. The original, which had an unsynchronized first gear, was followed by the all-synchromesh GT6 type, and the final version was the rationalized type also fitted to several other Triumph and Austin-Rover models.

Four-speed, non-synchro-first gear type

This design *originally* appeared in 1953 in the new SC Standard Eight, when it had wider ratios and a direct-action change with a long and willowy gear-lever.

Then, in 1957, it was used in the Standard Pennant, where it was treated to a remote-control change, and in further developed form it was then fitted to all versions of the Herald.

This gearbox was fitted to Spitfire Mks 1, 2 and 3 and can be recognized by the lack of first-gear synchromesh, and its reverse gear position, left and forward of the 1-2-3-4 gate. There was also a close-ratio version, fitted to the Vitesse 1600.

These were the details of 1960s types:

Internal ratios	Applications
1.00, 1.454, 2.460, 4.27, reverse 4.27:1 (Overdrive ratio 0.82:1)	Triumph Herald, Herald 1200 and Spitfire Mks 1, 2 and 3.
1.00, 1.254, 1.779, 2.932, reverse 2.932:1 (Overdrive ratio 0.82:1)	Triumph Vitesse 1600 (also homologated for competition Spitfires from 1964 to 1966)

Four-speed all-synchromesh type

This design was first developed for use in the Vitesse 2-litre and GT6 models, but wider-ratio versions were later adopted for the Spitfire and Toledo/1500TC family saloons.

In the car, it is recognized by the reverse gear position being to the left and forward of the 1-2-3-4 gate.

In general design it was similar to that of the non-synchro first type, but had a longer and stiffer casing.

Internal ratios	Applications
1.00, 1.254, 1.778, 2.65, reverse 3.10:1 (Overdrive ratio 0.80:1)	Triumph Vitesse 2-litre, GT6 and Dolomite 1850
1.00, 1.394, 2.158, 3.504, reverse 3.988:1 (Overdrive ratio 0.80:1)	Triumph Spitfire Mk IV, Toledo and 1500TC

Four-speed, all-synchromesh – single-rail type

This was a further-developed version of the all-synchromesh type already in use on Spitfire Mk IVs and all types of GT6. Although it retained the same internal ratios, it was given a revised single-rail selector mechanism and gearchange arrangement.

The same basic gearbox was also used in the Spitfire-engined MG Midget of 1974–1979, the Morris Marina and contemporary Triumph saloons. Compared with the earlier type, reverse gear position was to right and forward of the 1-2-3-4 gate. The Triumph ratios (*not* the MG or Morris ratios) were:

Internal ratios	Applications
1.00, 1.394, 2.158, 3.504, reverse 3.988:1 (Overdrive ratio 0.80:1)	Triumph Spitfire 1500, MG Midget (Triumph-engined type) and Dolomite 1300/1500 saloons

Motorsport footnote

Several different types of gearbox were used on the works Spitfires of 1964 to 1965:

** The standard wide-ratio gearboxes were never used in works-built competition cars. The ratios did not suit the peaky engines, and in any case they were not strong enough.

** The close-ratio non-synchro gearbox (Vitesse 1600-type) was used on the works rally Spitfires in the 1964 Alpine rally.

** The GT6-syle all-synchromesh gearbox was used on the works rally Spitfires from the 1964 Tour de France onwards, even though they could not be homologated...They were also used in the 1965 race cars.

** The larger TR4/Triumph 2000 type of gearbox, which was never fitted to production cars, was used in the 1964 Le Mans race cars, which ran as prototypes.

Rear axles

When the Triumph Herald was being designed in the late 1950s it was given independent rear suspension and a new chassis-mounted rear axle-differential assembly. The first cars were extremely low-geared with a 4.875:1 final-drive ratio.

The same basic layout was retained for all subsequent cars of the Herald/Vitesse/Spitfire/GT6 family; not all were interchangeable, and there were many differences between individual models.

Not only were there different final-drive ratios (as numerically high as 4.875:1 for the 948cc-engined Herald, as numerically low as 3.27:1 for the GT6), but there were several combinations of propeller-shaft flanges, pinion bearing sizes, output flanges and output shafts.

A chart assembled by Spitfire enthusiast C Eichoff, of Sweden, and published in the Triumph Sports Six's magazine *The Courier* once took two closely typed pages to define all the differences between all the axles. This is an invaluable document, but you'll have to join the TSSC to gain access to it!

The following chart (prepared by Triumph parts supply expert John Kipping and originally published in *The Courier*) shows how the various axles are related:

Triumph model	Axle ratio	Propshaft flange	Pinion bearing	Output shaft	Output flange
Spitfire Mk 1, 2 or 3 (to chassis FC120000)	4.11	S	S	S	S
Spitfire Mk 3 (from chassis FC120001	4.11	S	S	L	S
Spitfire Mk IV	3.89	L	L	L	L
Spitfire 1500	3.63	L	L	L	L
GT6	3.27	L	L	L	L
GT6	3.89	L	L	L	L

Triumph model	Axle ratio	Propshaft flange	Pinion bearing	Output shaft	Output flange
Herald 1200 (to chassis GA237600)	4.11	S	S	S	S
Herald 1200 (from chassis GA237601) and all 13/60s	4.11	S	S	L	S
Vitesse 1600	4.11	S	S	S	L
Vitesse 2-litre	3.89	L	L	L	L

Notes: These are the variables:

Flanges connecting the differential to the drive-shafts or the propeller-shaft – ½in or ⁹⁄₁₆ bolts (indicated as S for Small or L for Large).
Pinion bearings – original size or enlarged (S or L).
Differential output shafts (sometimes known as quarter-shafts) – original size (S, and rather weak) or enlarged (L, much more robust).
All 3.89:1, 3.63:1 and 3.27:1 rear axles are completely interchangeable in the various chassis, all having the largest and strongest specifications of components.
I have not listed 4.875:1 and 4.55:1 ratios as these were only fitted to 948cc-engined Heralds and are the weakest of the breed.

Chassis-frames
The backbone chassis-frame used as the foundation of Spitfire and GT6 models was unique to those cars; differences between the two cars were confined to mountings and braces to support different engine and radiator positions.
Heralds and Vitesses had entirely different frames. The only shared components were the bolt-on front suspension towers and the support brackets for the rear axle casings.

Front suspension and front brakes
Once the Spitfire and GT6 family was established, the whole separate-chassis Triumph family of cars shared the same basic front suspension layout and components.
There were several different braking installations (different discs and different calipers), and in general Spitfires and Heralds share the same components, while GT6s and Vitesse 2-litre models share an uprated installation.

Note: There are so many small differences between different types of Spitfire and GT6 that it would be folly to delve deeper in this Appendix. In all cases, restorers should arm themselves with the appropriate parts lists before beginning a rebuild.

APPENDIX E

Performance figures

Every variation on the Spitfire and GT6 theme was accurately tested by one or other of the most respected motoring magazines, so it is easy to compare one model with another.
With the single exception of the Spitfire Mk 3, Britain's *Autocar* tested all possible UK-market cars. For Spitfire Mk 3 figures, therefore, I turned to *Motor*. In later years, of course, those two magazines merged...
To give an idea of how the USA-specification cars suffered a

performance loss due to the power-sapping effect of exhaust emission regulations, I consulted *Road & Track*.

Except that the Spitfire Mk IV was slightly slower than the Spitfire Mk 3 (*Autocar* and *Motor* are both agreed about this), each type was slightly faster than the model it replaced. Incidentally, those Mk IV figures were not taken from a 'rogue' car; the same machine (TRW 857J) was later tested by *Motor* and recorded almost identical figures.

It's significant that while each of the overdrive-equipped Spitfires was faster in direct top than in overdrive top, the GT6s were more sensibly geared, and overdrive was effectively a fifth gear. On the Spitfire, it seems, overdrive was only meant as a cruising or economy gear – it did nothing to improve the performance.

	Spitfire Mk 1	Spitfire Mk 2	Spitfire Mk 3	Spitfire Mk IV	Spitfire 1500	Spitfire Mk IV (USA 1971)	Spitfire 1500 (USA 1973)	GT6 Mk 1	GT6 Mk 2	GT6 Mk 3	GT6 Mk 3 (USA 1973)
Mean maximum speed											
Overdrive top (mph)	–	90	94	87	97	–	–	106	107	–	–
Direct top (mph)	92	92	95	90	100	86	94	100	94	112	104
Acceleration (sec)											
0–30mph	5.0	4.7	4.3	4.8	3.8	4.5	4.7	3.6	3.5	3.9	4.4
0–40mph	7.6	7.0	6.8	7.3	6.3	7.2	7.2	5.9	5.2	5.5	–
0–50mph	10.9	11.0	10.1	11.0	8.8	11.3	10.9	8.5	7.2	7.7	9.3
0–60mph	17.3	15.5	14.5	16.2	13.2	15.9	15.4	12.0	10.0	10.1	12.6
0–70mph	25.8	21.8	20.7	22.9	18.1	25.0	21.6	15.6	13.7	14.0	–
0–80mph	36.9	33.6	30.7	33.3	25.3	40.2	31.8	21.2	18.2	18.4	23.4
0–90mph	–	–	49.3	–	38.7	–	–	31.3	26.2	24.5	–
0–100mph	–	–	–	–	–	–	–	–	39.3	35.8	–
Standing ¼-mile (sec)	20.9	20.0	19.6	20.6	19.1	21.0	20.2	18.5	17.3	17.4	19.6
Direct top gear accel (sec)											
10–30mph	–	–	–	–	–	–	–	–	7.8	–	–
20–40mph	13.5	13.9	10.5	12.4	11.2	–	–	6.7	6.5	8.6	–
30–50mph	13.6	12.5	11.1	11.7	10.0	–	–	6.9	6.7	7.8	–
40–60mph	13.7	12.5	11.0	12.6	10.3	–	–	7.9	6.9	8.3	–
50–70mph	15.8	14.6	12.8	16.3	12.1	–	–	8.5	7.9	9.2	–
60–80mph	19.6	20.3	16.1	23.0	15.0	–	–	10.0	9.5	10.1	–
70–90mph	–	–	–	25.4	21.0	–	–	16.1	13.2	11.7	–
80–100mph	–	–	–	–	–	–	–	–	–	16.9	–
Overall fuel consumption (mpg)	31.2	29.8	32.8	32.1	29.2	–	–	20.2	25.2	27.6	–
Typical fuel consumption (mpg)	33	34	39	35	32	36	30	24	28	28	25
Kerb weight (lb)	1,589	1,635	1,736	1,717	1,780	1,795	1,735	1,964	1,988	2,023	2,025
Original test published	1962	1966	1967	1971	1975	1971	1973	1967	1969	1971	1973